Enlarging the EU Eastwards

CHATHAM HOUSE PAPERS

A European Programme Publication
Programme Head: Dr Kirsty Hughes

The Royal Institute of International Affairs, at Chatham House in London, has provided an impartial forum for discussion and debate on current international issues for over 75 years. Its resident research fellows, specialized information resources, and range of publications, conferences, and meetings span the fields of international politics, economics, and security. The Institute is independent of government.

Chatham House Papers are short monographs on current policy problems which have been commissioned by the RIIA. In preparing the papers, authors are advised by a study group of experts convened by the RIIA, and publication of a paper indicates that the Institute regards it as an authoritative contribution to the public debate. The Institute does not, however, hold opinions of its own; the views expressed in this publication are the responsibility of the authors.

CHATHAM HOUSE PAPERS

Enlarging the EU Eastwards

Heather Grabbe and Kirsty Hughes

THE ROYAL INSTITUTE
OF INTERNATIONAL
AFFAIRS

Pinter
A Cassell Imprint
Wellington House, 125 Strand, London WC2R 0BB, United Kingdom
PO Box 605, Herndon, VA 20172, USA

First published in 1998

British Library Cataloguing in Publication Data
A CIP catalogue record for this book is available from the British Library

Library of Congress Cataloging in Publication Data
A CIP catalogue record for this book is available from the Library of Congress

ISBN 1-85567-526-9 (Paperback)
      1-85567-525-0 (Hardback)

Typeset by Koinonia Limited
Printed and bound in Great Britain by
Biddles Limited, Guildford and King's Lynn

Contents

Acknowledgments

We have benefited from discussions with a very large number of people; we would like to thank in particular the members of a Chatham House Study Group and participants in various European Programme round-tables and workshops on enlargement. We are also grateful to the large number of policy-makers and analysts across the EU and in central and eastern Europe who have discussed enlargement and related issues with us; they are not, of course, responsible for the views expressed here.

December 1997   Heather Grabbe
Kirsty Hughes

About the authors

Heather Grabbe is Research Fellow in the European Programme at the Royal Institute of International Affairs. She was previously International Economics and Western Europe Editor at Oxford Analytica.

Dr Kirsty Hughes is Head of the European Programme at the Royal Institute of International Affairs. From 1992 to 1995 she was Head of the European Industrial Development Group at the Policy Studies Institute.

Abbreviations

CAP	Common Agricultural Policy
CEE	central and eastern Europe/European
CMEA	Council for Mutual Economic Assistance (Comecon)
EBRD	European Bank for Reconstruction and Development
ECU	European Currency Unit
EEA	European Economic Area
EFTA	European Free Trade Association
EMU	Economic and Monetary Union
EU	European Union
FDI	foreign direct investment
GDP	gross domestic product
GNP	gross national product
IGC	Intergovernmental Conference
NATO	North Atlantic Treaty Organization
OECD	Organization for Economic Cooperation and Development
PPP	purchasing power parity
QMV	qualified majority voting
SMEs	small and medium-sized enterprises
WEU	Western European Union
WTO	World Trade Organization

Map of Europe

Chapter 1

Introduction

For four decades, the peoples of western and eastern Europe experienced parallel but very different systems of integration, the one contributing to increasing stability and prosperity, the other enforced by Soviet domination. The revolutions of 1989 and 1991 have offered the chance to turn Cold War threats into opportunities by integrating the countries of central and eastern Europe (CEE) into the European Union (EU). Eastward enlargement of the EU is inspired partly by a sense of historical opportunity; it is not motivated just by the logic of political, economic and security interests on both sides, but has an emotional and moral dimension in reuniting Europe and making up for the painful divisions of Yalta.

Integrating these very different countries into the EU presents an unprecedented challenge. There are currently ten applicants for membership from central and eastern Europe: Bulgaria, the Czech Republic, Estonia, Hungary, Latvia, Lithuania, Poland, Romania, Slovakia and Slovenia. In absorbing all ten countries, the EU would add nearly a third to its population but only 4%[1] to its GDP, and average per capita GDP in the CEE-10 is only one-third of the average EU level.[2] Moreover, these countries are still in the process of transforming their economies and societies after nearly half a century of central planning and Soviet domination. The requirements of membership present a major challenge for countries in transition because they are taking on a much more complex *acquis communautaire* from a lower starting point than any previous applicant.

[1] At current market prices.
[2] On a purchasing power parity (PPP) basis.

1

At the same time as CEE is transforming itself, the EU is becoming increasingly complex as it moves towards monetary union and further integration in other areas, particularly justice and home affairs. These developments make the EU a moving target for applicants trying to jump on board, and they complicate the process of enlargement because of their impact on the political environment in the EU. The single currency is particularly important in this respect; efforts to achieve monetary union have already affected the political environment for the Community budget because member states straining to meet the convergence criteria are extremely reluctant to extend significant transfers to CEE. In addition, any serious difficulties concerning the single currency could inhibit the process of enlargement.

Enlarging the EU eastwards will have major political, economic and security implications, and the process is likely to be long and complex. An enlarged EU will have to cope with much more diversity in economic circumstances and political goals as well as with the increase in numbers. These changes will take place over a number of years, because the applicants will not all join at the same time, but the cumulative effect will be a fundamental change in the EU's functioning, and possibly in its capacities as well. For this reason, it is essential that the EU develop a strategic overview of what it should look like in 10–15 years' time and with 25 or more members. As yet, no such overview exists, and the EU has taken a largely 'business as usual' approach to this enlargement.

In addition to making the overall outcome even more uncertain, this lack of strategy fails to give the EU sufficient momentum to prepare itself for enlargement. EU member states have a long history of not dealing with major challenges until such matters are forced to the top of the political agenda by circumstances. Enlargement is no exception: at present there is no sense of urgency about it because there is no immediate crisis concerning CEE. Although EU politicians make frequent rhetorical references to their commitment to enlargement, the minimal results of the Intergovernmental Conference that ended in Amsterdam in June 1997 show how unwilling they are to take the difficult decisions needed to manage the process successfully. This reluctance reflects member states' widely varying attitudes towards enlargement, in terms of both means (enlargement policies) and ends (how far the EU should extend, and how it should adapt itself).

As a result, there is a major risk that the EU will fail to reform its institutions and policies sufficiently coherently to allow it to continue to function effectively after enlargement. Incorporating such a large number of new members, albeit in stages, will inevitably affect the political dynamics of the EU; it might make the EU too cumbersome, and presage the onset of a new bout of 'Eurosclerosis', if decision-making processes cannot cope. However, there is a wide variety of views across both current and prospective member states as to how to deal with this risk: some see it as a reason for furthering integration and transferring more responsibilities up to Community level, whereas others see the answer in making the EU more flexible or reducing the scope of EU-level decision-making. With regard to the policies delivered through the Community budget, no member state is prepared to accept the costs of extending current levels of transfers to new CEE members. Both net contributors and net recipients are already arguing about the relatively small sums proposed for the next financial perspective.

The next few years will see steps taken towards addressing these issues. The start of negotiations in the first half of 1998 with at least some of the applicants will bring many of the questions into perspective and should provide more momentum to the process; there is also a new budget for 2000 onwards to be negotiated. The European Commission has laid out key options for handling negotiations, and for reforming EU policies, in its 'Agenda 2000' proposals. It has also produced *avis* (or opinions) on all the applicants, looking at their progress in transition and readiness for membership. These documents are already stimulating debate among member states and will be a key influence on their decisions about how to manage the enlargement process.

The structure of this book

This book provides an analytical overview of the political, economic and security dimensions of enlargement. It starts with an analysis of EU and CEE motivations for enlargement (see below), discussing the wide range of interests and concerns driving countries' attitudes towards the enlargement process, and the wider regional context.

Chapter 2 considers the process of integration between the EU and the CEE applicants already under way, through interregional trade and investment flows, in advance of formal accession. It is clear that this integration is growing rapidly, but it is uneven across EU member states, with Germany playing by far the most prominent role in both trade and foreign direct investment (FDI). This unevenness may have implications for the political economy of enlargement, but the chapter concludes that many of the economic effects of enlargement are likely to be felt in advance of accession, so its main significance could lie more in the political and security dimensions.

In addition to trade relations, the EU has developed a set of processes designed to prepare applicants for membership through its 'pre-accession strategy', and these are covered in Chapter 3. There is a general consensus across the EU and CEE that this strategy now needs strengthening for the applicants, particularly in the light of their wide-ranging needs in preparing for accession. Chapter 4 considers the Commission's *avis* on the ten applicants and their economic and political transitions, including how far they are from EU norms. The issues involved in opening negotiations in 1998 and the substantive issues that will come under discussion are covered in Chapter 5, along with an assessment of the Commission's proposals for reinforcing the pre-accession strategy presented in Agenda 2000.

Chapter 6 provides an overview of applicant country views on the enlargement process; CEE political debates and public opinion on EU membership are already developing in a way that permits some preliminary analysis of emerging views. On the EU side, discussion of the reforms needed for enlargement is already under way, but progress is likely to be slow. Chapter 7 considers the options for EU policies and institutions, including the Commission's proposals for the EU budget to run from 2000.

Chapter 8 considers the implications of enlargement for security and the external relations of both existing and prospective member states. The parallel but uncoordinated process of NATO expansion raises important questions about how the enlarged EU will deal with its own security dimension and its relations with its regional neighbours as the CEE applicants join. The final chapter brings together the main conclusions.

Why enlarge the EU?

EU member state views

All EU members have an interest in ensuring that the large region on their doorstep is stable, secure and prosperous. Since the Copenhagen European Council in 1993, which formally committed the EU to the principle of enlargement to all ten CEE applicants, member states have generally supported enlargement as a way of promoting stability and prosperity in Europe by bringing the CEE countries into the EU's frameworks of economic and political integration. However, individual member states' degree of commitment to the process is open to question; there is considerable debate about how fast enlargement should proceed and how far eastwards it should go.

Member states' interests in enlargement vary according to their proximity to potential areas of instability on the peripheries of the EU, their economic integration with CEE and their historical links with particular countries. There is also a wide range of views about how to reform EU policies and institutions to fit what could eventually be 25 or more members.

EU countries in close geographical proximity to CEE tend both to have more immediate concerns about security and stability, and in many cases to have closer economic ties than the rest of the EU. This applies to the Scandinavian member states, Finland, Germany, Austria, Greece and, to a lesser extent, Italy. Some countries further from the EU's eastern border have also emphasized the importance of stability and security in the new Europe, most notably the UK.

Other countries are much more ambivalent about enlargement. France is notably so, notwithstanding its leaders' public rhetoric about accession of Poland, Hungary and the Czech Republic by 2000. The emergence of a reunified Germany with strong economic ties in CEE implies a major shift in the European centre of gravity which enlargement will reinforce. There is perhaps an implicit Franco-German deal here: economic and monetary union in return for at least some enlargement. Further south, Spain and Portugal have few reasons to express positive interest in enlargement; their immediate concern is to participate in the single currency from the start and they want to protect budgetary transfers that might be threatened by enlargement. Nor is enlargement strongly supported by small and traditionally integrationist countries such as Belgium and Luxembourg.

Geo-political and economic interests affect not only overall policy stances on enlargement but also views on which CEE countries are most important. Despite the general stress on equal treatment and objective criteria, it is widely recognized that the Scandinavian countries are particularly concerned about stabilizing the three Baltic applicants, while Germany is more focused on Poland followed by the Czech Republic and Hungary, and further south Greece will have an especial interest in successful transition in Bulgaria and Romania. The extent to which all EU member states are really committed to bringing in all ten of the applicants is open to doubt. Furthermore, although historical experience may lead some member states to recognize the moral dimension of enlargement – notably the way in which accession helped to consolidate democratization in Greece, Portugal and Spain – this is unlikely to override political and economic interests.

The 15 EU countries have very different degrees of economic integration with CEE at present (see Chapter 2), and their economic interests in enlargement are likely to continue to vary considerably in the medium term. Economic ties may lead to more support for enlargement, particularly if enlarging the Single Market to the East is expected to yield economic benefits to the EU. But economic integration may not just encourage positive views about enlargement in national politics. There are also domestic political sensibilities in some member states about the potential for CEE accessions to cause capital outflows and relocation of production from western Europe, as well as migration of workers from the East. A number of these issues are already becoming significant in domestic political debate in Germany and Austria, causing tensions in their enlargement policies; both have economic and security interests in their eastern neighbours, but their political debates also reflect fears about potential consequences of enlargement, such as wage competition and migration. There are indications that Germany would be content to see a fairly slow process of enlargement.

Member states' motivations and attitudes to enlargement are also affected by their attitudes towards European integration and their views on the EU's institutional and policy development (see Chapter 7). Many member states have expressed the view that enlargement must not impede the effective functioning of the EU, and there have been widespread suspicions that the UK's support for enlargement (particularly under the previous Conservative government) reflected a desire to see a weaker, looser EU rather than genuine geopolitical and security concerns. France, Belgium and Italy issued a joint declaration after the Amsterdam Treaty was signed calling for more institutional reform prior to the first accessions, seeming to make this a prerequisite for enlargement. Thus, although UK support for enlargement may be seen as potentially undermining integration, other member states' support for integration might undermine the enlargement process.

CEE motivations

Across central and eastern Europe there has been enthusiasm for joining international organizations to facilitate and consolidate re-integration into the world economy and a departure from the Soviet sphere of influence. Fulfilling conditions to join international bodies has been helpful in guiding the opening of economies and encouraging the development of democratic institutions, but the symbolism of being accepted by organizations from the Council of Europe to the World Trade Organization is equally important. These various memberships are a demonstration of post-communist societies' emergence as sovereign states in the international arena, both to the world and to their own populations. For countries that are also building new nationhood as independent states, such as Slovakia, Slovenia and the Baltic states, acceptance by international organizations is often seen as an affirmation of their independence and sovereignty, as well as their success in transition.

The European Union and NATO are seen as the most important institutions to join, both because of the practical benefits of membership and also because of what they represent. Indeed, the process of Euro-Atlantic integration is the foreign policy priority of all ten applicants. The main attraction of NATO is the hard security guarantee it offers, and integration into its structures will be fairly fast for the three countries so far invited to join. Joining the EU is a much more complex process, however, given its much broader scope and aims. Debate has hardly started yet about its implications in most candidate countries, but a number of issues could take on more importance as negotiations begin and an awareness of the EU's activities grows among political elites and public opinion (see Chapter 6).

The central foreign policy goal in all ten applicants from the early years of transition was the desire to 'return to Europe', and in most countries the political debate has not yet moved much beyond this level. There is a strong sense that the process of joining the European Union is an inevitable one, both arising from and reaffirming their status as modern European states. For this reason, political actors tend to cite the experience of Greece, Spain and Portugal in joining the EU when they became democracies, and hardly ever refer to the alternative arrangements negotiated by Switzerland and Norway. In policy documents and academic research, there are frequent references to the countries' histories in Europe and to geographical positions between East and West. There is even a growing tendency for all of the applicants, even those farthest east, south and north, to claim to be 'central European' countries.

Arguments in favour of joining the EU tend to be presented in terms of the logic of historical precedent, geographical position and psychological need. Potential economic benefits through trade, investment and transfers tend to be a secondary argument behind these primary reasons for acceding. Ensuring the full opening of markets for all products, including agriculture, is an important part of economic motivations. As yet, there is hardly any disagreement with the frequent statements that full membership is the only option. This seems to reflect a strong belief that membership of the EU will fulfil a need of CEE countries to feel once more part of Europe, as well as offering concrete benefits.

The security and foreign policy implications of EU membership are particularly important in Poland and the Baltic states, although this aspect is seen more in terms of the EU being a community of states rather than because of any hopes for the development of a common foreign and security policy. The implicit security guarantee that is effectively part of EU membership is very important; although there is no formal pact to defend one another, the emphasis on solidarity and ever-closer integration within the Union offers reassurance that EU states, many of which are NATO members, will react to external aggression threatening fellow members in CEE. Moving into the EU is an important part of moving decisively out of the Russian sphere of influence, particularly for the Baltic states.

The strength of this widespread feeling puts a heavy burden on the process of EU accession to deliver the security and political benefits expected of it, particularly given the potential costs of alignment with EU norms and taking on the whole *acquis communautaire*. The experience of member states suggests that countries which joined primarily for economic reasons (such as the UK, Sweden and Denmark) have experienced greater long-run scepticism about European integration than those with motives such as affirming their identity as small, independent states (Ireland, Luxembourg and Belgium, for example) or overcoming historical conflicts (Germany, France and Italy, for example). In the long run, support for the EU could strengthen if the CEE countries succeed in gaining their political goals.

The potential for financial transfers from the Community budget is generally not a central motivation, although transfers could play a greater role in political debates as membership draws closer. Estonian and Czech leaders have stated publicly that their countries will not need transfers, but not always to the approval of the rest of their political establishments. The prospect of getting them does not yet seem to play a strong role in the debate in Slovenia or the other Baltic states either, but there are expectations that this will become more important once the scale of potential transfers becomes clearer. Overall, transfers are seen by many CEE policy-makers and journalists as a useful way of encouraging public support for accession. In predominantly agricultural countries such as

Poland, Romania and Bulgaria, transfers to farmers could play a particularly important role. The main issue at present seems to be the principle of equal treatment rather than the scale of the transfers; many policymakers argue that, if other member states have full access to EU policies, so should they. Nevertheless, transfers to compare with those to the current EU-15 are unlikely (see Chapter 6).

The regional context

Eastward enlargement will have an impact beyond its profound effects on the EU and the applicants. Extending the borders of the EU will increase its weight in the region, as well as globally, in areas such as trade negotiations. Although the process of enlargement may help to stabilize the applicants and guide their post-communist transitions, the EU will face difficult strategic issues on its new eastern and southern frontiers, and these may themselves be complicated by the EU's expansion (see Chapter 8).

There is also a Mediterranean dimension to the process of enlargement. In addition to the CEE applicants, the EU has committed itself to opening negotiations with Cyprus in 1998. This book is about the eastward enlargement of the EU, so it does not deal with the complex issues raised by the applications of Cyprus and Turkey; however, it is important to point out their implications for eastward enlargement.

The European Commission published a favourable opinion on the Cypriot application in 1993; Malta also received a favourable opinion, but subsequently suspended its application for membership following a change of government. The EU is pledged to negotiate accession terms with the Cypriot government even in the absence of a resolution to the division of the island; member states are currently seeking a way of including a delegation from the northern part of the island in this process. There are deep divisions of opinion among member states about the circumstances under which Cyprus could become a member. Greece has threatened to veto eastward enlargement if Cyprus is not admitted too; however, the likelihood of other member states agreeing to the accession of a divided island is very low.

Relations with Turkey are also an issue in enlargement, because of its role in the Cypriot question and because its own application to join the EU remains on the table. There are considerable concerns on the Turkish side that ties should be upgraded, which led to calls in Ankara for a veto over NATO expansion if the EU did not actively reconsider its application.

Member states are divided about how best to deal with Turkish relations in the context of enlargement, and the possibility of including Turkey in a standing European Conference has provoked different reactions (see Chapter 5).

In the next decade the EU could receive further applications from the east and south: in particular, Ukraine, Moldova, Albania and the remaining former Yugoslav republics might apply. This prospect raises further difficult challenges for the EU in considering notions of solidarity and identity in Europe: how far can the EU extend before it loses its cohesion and effectiveness? How can EU members, both old and new, develop constructive relations with neighbours that remain far from the prospect of membership?

Other questions also arise, even just in contemplating the initial eastward enlargement. Can the EU develop appropriate institutions and policies to unite its members in seeking common goals? Will the EU be able to confront new political, economic and security challenges sufficiently well to remain relevant to its members? These wider questions are becoming increasingly urgent, not just because of enlargement, and there is a risk that member states will remain too focused on national preferences in reforming EU institutions and policies to address them properly.

Overall, member states' differing interests in and degrees of commitment to enlargement mean that keeping the process on track and maintaining its momentum will require astute political bargaining and complex alliances between member states, even before considering the challenges faced by the applicants. Who will provide the political skills to give the leadership required? The Commission alone cannot drive enlargement forward politically. Although there is a role for the UK and the Nordic countries here, Germany has to be a central part of the answer. Successful enlargement demands strategic leadership; whether it will emerge is currently an open question.

Chapter 2

East-West economic integration and enlargement

Introduction

As their main source of trade, aid and investment, the EU is the key economic partner for CEE countries, and economic interests are one of their motivations for joining. Economic interpenetration between the EU and CEE economies has so far been rapid, with the CEE countries quickly reorienting their trade from CMEA markets to the EU in the early years of transition. However, the importance of this integration has been somewhat asymmetric because the small CEE economies are much less important as trading partners for the EU countries. Moreover, degrees of economic involvement with the CEE region vary considerably across the EU-15, making economic interests for all but a few EU member states quite small.

This chapter analyses in detail trade and investment flows between the EU and CEE countries to examine how much economic integration is happening prior to accession, and to explore the different economic interests of individual CEE and EU countries. There is a detailed analysis of data on trade and investment flows between the EU and the CEE applicants since 1989, and a discussion of potential future trends in integration. The conclusion from the evidence presented is that, because of the substantial degree of economic integration already being achieved, many of the potential economic benefits of enlargement may in fact be realized prior to accession.

Table 2.1: Annual rate of growth in EU–CEE trade, 1989–95

	% growth over previous year							% growth
	1989	*1990*	*1991*	*1992*	*1993*	*1994*	*1995*	*1989–95*
EU-12 exports to CEE-6	16	47	16	28	9	19	38	131
EU-12 imports from CEE-6	8	30	16	22	-3	31	40	185

Source: own calculations based on IMF.

Trade

Trade growth between the two regions has been very dynamic since 1989. As is shown in Table 2.1, exports to the CEE-6[1] from the EU grew by an average of 25% per year in the first seven years of transition, and imports from CEE countries by 21%, although they fluctuated considerably from year to year. Factors behind this fluctuation include the recession of the early 1990s in western Europe, the plunge and then gradual recovery of output in CEE after the initial shock of transition, and trade liberalization on both sides.

Similar fluctuations in year-on-year growth can be seen in CEE trade with the world. Overall growth in CEE trade outside the EU was much slower between 1989 and 1994, with only a 37% increase in exports, but 1995 saw exports jump by one-third again. Lower levels of growth until 1995 reflect the extent to which the collapse of the CMEA, including the drop in trade with East Germany and the former Soviet Union, led to a much greater reorientation of trade towards western Europe than towards the rest of the world. For example, absolute trade flows between CEE and the United States, the world's largest trader, remain small by comparison with the EU's involvement.

A more detailed picture of the reorientation of CEE trade after 1989 is provided in Table 2.2. By 1994 the EU had become the most important market for CEE exports, accounting for over half of the total. In part, the rapidity of the re-orientation is accounted for by the low base from which EU–CEE trade grew. The Europe Agreements also played a role by providing a framework for continued liberalization and locking both sides into a time frame for reducing trade barriers (see Chapter 3). However,

---

[1] CEE-6 are Bulgaria, Czech Republic, Hungary, Poland, Romania and Slovakia. The Baltic states and Slovenia are excluded from all 1989 totals because their trade was not recorded separately by the IMF prior to their independence.

Table 2.2: Reorientation of CEE-6 trade: exports, 1989–95 (%)

	1989	1995
CEE exports to:		
Former CMEA[a]	47	23
EU-15	35	63
USA	2	2
Japan	1	1
Rest of the world	15	11

[a] These data should be taken as indicative rather than precise because of disparities in the methodology used (notably the rouble conversion rate and eastern Germany's position). *Source:* CEC 1997.

CMEA-imposed trade patterns were still being unwound for some years, so it is not yet clear to what extent the re-orientation is primarily in accordance with comparative advantage, and to what extent it is 'distress trade' diverted from eastern markets (see Drábek and Smith 1995).

Despite this growth and reorientation, however, trade with CEE countries still accounts for less than 10% of total extra-EU trade, primarily because these economies are still so small in comparison with the EU. However, the region takes a greater share of EU exports than does Japan, and trade is still growing rapidly. Moreover, significant further expansion is likely in line with growth in GDP and incomes in CEE, whereas many of the EU's other markets are at or are reaching maturity. From this point of view, the CEE countries represent an important market with considerable potential for the EU.

Among individual CEE countries, Poland accounted for about 30% of total trade with the EU in 1995, the Czech Republic around 20%, Hungary 16% and Slovenia 10%. These top four countries thus account for over three-quarters of total exports and imports, with the others well behind, reflecting differences between the CEE countries in terms of size, but also in terms of levels of economic development and degrees of openness to trade.

For the individual EU countries, there are marked differences in the importance of CEE trade in their total trade (see Table 2.3). For Austria and Greece, CEE trade accounts for a considerable share of total extra-EU trade, and it is also quite significant for Germany and Finland. At the other end of the scale, however, for six out of the 15 member states, the CEE share is less than 5%. With the exception of Greece, the cohesion

13

Table 2.3: CEE Share of extra-EU trade in 1995 (%)[a]

	Exports	Imports
Austria	27.2	28.1
Greece	19.9	11.7
Germany	13.9	15.6
Finland	13.4	9.9
Italy	9.6	8.7
Netherlands	8.5	4.3
Denmark	7.5	9.7
Sweden	6.6	7.9
Belgium-Luxembourg	4.8	3.6
France	4.3	4.1
Spain	4.3	3.8
United Kingdom	4.0	2.9
Ireland	3.5	1.5
Portugal	2.2	2.0
EU-15 total	9.1	8.2

[a] The CEE countries' share of extra-EU trade is significantly larger in 1995 then it was in 1994, primarily because the 1995 figure for total extra-EU trade excludes Austria, Finland and Sweden, which had by then joined the EU. Because the total extra-EU trade for each country is smaller, CEE trade appears proportionately larger.
Source: own calculations based on *Eurostat* (various issues) and IMF.

Table 2.4: Shares of main EU exporters to CEE countries, 1989 and 1995

	% of EU-15 exports to CEE-6	
	1989	1995
Germany	36.05	51.43
Italy	15.53	11.75
Austria	9.79	7.87
France	9.83	5.84
United Kingdom	7.79	5.47
Netherlands	5.51	3.72
Other	25.30	21.79
Total	100.00	100.00

Source: own calculations based on IMF.

Table 2.5: EU-15 share of world exports to CEE countries in 1995

	%
Slovenia	79
Poland	69
Hungary	67
Czech Republic	66
Estonia	65
Bulgaria	56
Romania	54
Latvia	45
Slovakia	44
Lithuania	37
CEE total	58

Source: own calculations based on IMF.

countries have very small levels of trade with CEE. Economic interests in CEE thus vary considerably across the EU-15, which may have implications for the political economy of enlargement.

The diversity in the shares taken by the different EU members in trade with the CEE region is shown in Table 2.4. Germany accounted for by far the largest share of CEE trade among EU countries in 1989, although this was in the context of very low levels of overall EU trade with the region in 1995. Despite the strong growth in overall trade flows and the change in economic relations with CEE, Germany still dominates trade, accounting for half of total EU exports to the region. The UK's share of CEE trade is particularly low in comparison with its share of world trade (see Grabbe 1997). The US share of CEE trade is also small, particularly given that it has the largest share of world trade, although the USA is a much more significant source of FDI in the CEE region (as discussed below).

Economic interpenetration between the two regions is asymmetric, with the EU having less of an economic interest in CEE than vice versa. For the CEE countries, trade with the EU-15 is more important than trade with any other region (see Table 2.5), including intra-CEE trade. The EU accounts for more than half of total imports into the region, and for two-thirds of imports for five of the CEE-10. However, as Table 2.5 shows, degrees of trade dependence on the EU vary across the CEE-10.

Table 2.6: Top five EU exporters to individual CEE countries in 1995 ($m)

Poland		Hungary		Czech Republic		Slovakia	
EU-15 total	19,624	EU-15 total	10,713	EU-15 total	14,994	EU-15 total	3,977
Germany	8,876	Germany	4,912	Germany	8,265	Czech Republic	2,811
Italy	2,518	Austria	1,512	Slovakia	2,817	Germany	2,156
Netherlands	1,377	Italy	1,415	Austria	1,477	Italy	513
United Kingdom	1,489	Russia	823	Italy	1,329	Austria	474
France	1,407	France	674	France	969	Poland	346

Slovenia		Estonia		Latvia		Lithuania	
EU-15 total	6,628	EU-15 total	1,857	EU-15 total	1,162	EU-15 total	1,324
Germany	2,195	Finland	943	Germany	414	Germany	537
Italy	1,922	Sweden	295	Russia	320	Russia	352
Croatia	871	Germany	259	Sweden	133	Ukraine	250
Austria	834	Russia	250	Netherlands	127	Finland	117
France	734	Lithuania	111	Lithuania	72	Sweden	108

Romania		Bulgaria	
EU-15 total	4,748	EU-15 total	2,754
Germany	1,795	Germany	930
Italy	1,284	Greece	551
France	484	Russia	429
Turkey	341	Italy	426
United Kingdom	279	Turkey	365

Source: own calculations based on IMF.

Table 2.6 demonstrates in more detail the enormous importance of EU members in CEE trade by showing the top five exporters world-wide to each of the CEE economies, and the EU-15 total. Germany is the single most important trading partner for eight of the ten, often many times larger than the second most important.[2] For the central European countries, Italy, Austria and France are the other main EU trading partners. The three Baltic economies trade much more with the Scandinavian EU members and Russia than do the others; Latvia and Lithuania retain a considerably larger proportion of their trade with Russia, while Finland provides over half of Estonia's EU imports. Bulgaria and Romania receive more of their imports from Turkey than the others, and Bulgaria conducts a much higher proportion of its trade with Greece.

The overall trade balance is a large net surplus for the EU, despite the asymmetry of the Europe Agreements in lifting restrictions on CEE exports first.[3] Interpretation of this surplus is a subject of considerable debate. It has been taken to demonstrate restrictions on CEE exports imposed by the trade regime (Nuti 1997; Inotai 1994), and, whatever economic effects lie behind them, the trade deficits have been seen in CEE political debates as an indication of the EU's lack of generosity in opening its markets, particularly for agricultural products.

Even though nearly all restrictions on trade in industrial goods have now been removed, the trade imbalance has continued to grow. However, contingent protection provisions remain which may have had a 'chilling effect' on potential CEE exporters who were contemplating entering EU markets but were put off because of fears of becoming the target of an anti-dumping or safeguard action. Other explanations for the trade imbalances have been put forward as well. One factor seems to be CEE imports of capital and intermediate goods to replace capital stock and underpin restructuring during transition, although some of these may have been for consumption. Varying levels of competitiveness in different sectors in the CEE countries also play a role, as do exchange rate fluctuations. All of these factors are likely to have had an impact, and it is difficult to disentangle the relative effects of each on the trade balances.

Behind the aggregate EU surplus lie important differences in the trade performance of individual EU members. The matrix of net trade balances (see Table 2.7) that emerges from the IMF data shows a mixed picture of

[2] The profile for imports is very similar to that for exports.
[3] The trade regime under the Europe Agreements is discussed in Chapter 3.

Table 2.7: EU net trade balances with CEE in 1995

	Poland	Hungary	Czech Republic	Slovakia	Slovenia	Estonia	Latvia	Lithuania	Romania	Bulgaria	CEE-10
Austria	133	79	220	37	246	6	16	7	110	65	919
Belgium-Luxembourg	77	55	98	10	59	14	10	0	-10	21	334
Denmark	-180	42	64	19	-4	3	18	2	25	7	-4
Finland	203	106	72	4	10	591	174	85	8	35	1,288
France	381	145	499	64	-37	0	-5	-26	26	-9	1,038
Germany	196	83	867	-41	-346	82	8	110	291	370	1,620
Greece	-33	-5	-46	-12	-25	1	3	5	-74	153	-33
Ireland	65	51	76	10	11	7	2	2	11	7	242
Italy	1,290	143	509	-44	753	36	27	20	-86	-78	2,570
Netherlands	441	103	241	21	90	-63	-184	-71	-12	3	569
Portugal	-22	17	-16	0	-11	-2	-3	-5	-6	-21	-69
Spain	118	-237	89	8	149	-1	3	5	-50	-116	-32
Sweden	188	145	104	-13	27	49	-1	-8	21	18	530
United Kingdom	482	-120	383	16	12	-130	-206	-196	3	-23	221
Total EU-15	3,339	607	3160	79	934	593	-138	-70	257	432	9,193

Source: own calculations based on IMF.

bilateral balances, but overall trade surpluses for 11 of the 15 EU countries.[4] All but two of the CEE-10 show trade deficits with the EU countries, adding to concerns about their balance-of-payments positions and competitiveness. However, the diverse picture of bilateral net trade balances suggests that there is a variety of determinants rather than a simple explanation.

This matrix has a number of possible implications for the political economy of enlargement on both sides. Most EU countries show a surplus in trade with most CEE countries; the exceptions are Portugal, Greece, Spain and Denmark. The relatively worse trade performance of these countries and the small size of their overall trade with CEE could have an effect on perceptions of the economic costs and benefits of enlargement; however, national political debate on this issue has so far been overshadowed by other concerns about enlargement, including its potential budgetary impact.

In summary, the geographical reorientation of trade towards the EU since 1989 has been rapid, as has overall growth, and Germany now accounts for half of all EU exports to and imports from CEE. Although the CEE countries' trading partners have changed, however, the commodities they are exporting do not appear to have altered much. OECD data and national data from the CEE statistical offices for 1989–95 analysed by the authors seem to support the arguments advanced elsewhere (Halpern 1995, Drábek and Smith 1995, Takla 1996) that the structure of trade, particularly exports, has changed remarkably little in the context of dramatic growth and reorientation. A number of different explanations have been offered for the lack of major change, centring on the deterrent effect of contingent protection provisions on investment in the production of new goods (Hamilton and Winters 1992) and restrictions on CEE exports of sensitive products (see Messerlin 1992, Rollo and Smith 1993).

However, a much more detailed breakdown of the commodity composition of trade is needed to disentangle the effects of the trade regime from other factors, most notably in the macroeconomic environment and the process of economic transition. Two major constituents of the initial macroeconomic context are recession in western Europe in the early 1990s, which reduced aggregate demand (Drábek and Smith 1995), and the collapse in output during those years in the East, which may have had a deterrent effect on new ventures in CEE.

[4] Like the other figures in this chapter, this matrix is calculated from IMF data on bilateral trade whose source is EU national statistics; data from Eurostat and other sources result in a slightly different pattern of bilateral balances.

19

The context of transition matters too, as a slow start to industrial restructuring in many of the associated countries (Estrin 1994) and the relatively low level of foreign investment until the end of 1993 in most CEE countries apart from Hungary are also likely to have played a role in continuing previous patterns of commodity exports.

It is not clear to what extent current patterns of trade reflect long-run patterns of comparative advantage (see contributions to Hughes and Hare 1992, Faini and Portes 1995). It is still too early to tell how far current export patterns indicate distortions owing to past trading relationships and the legacy of planning regimes and how much they are responses to international competition and industrial restructuring. However, it is interesting to note that there is evidence that the structure of imports by CEE shifted radically, showing a reduction in intermediate and investment goods and an increase in consumption goods (Faini and Portes 1995).

Foreign direct investment

With regard to investment, there is a similar concentration on particular countries. FDI inflows into central and eastern Europe were relatively low at the start of transition, but they have risen substantially subsequently (see Estrin et al. 1997 for a more detailed discussion). Inflows into the CEE-10 countries account for most of the inflows into transition economies at more than 80%, with the other transition economies, including Russia and the CIS, accounting for about 20%. Among the CEE-10, Hungary, Poland and the Czech Republic have received the bulk of the inflows, with over two-thirds of the total. Data on FDI in central and eastern Europe have not been entirely reliable, and in the early years of transition there were disagreements between international data sources and national data; in particular, there were problems with investments by multinationals being recorded as coming from their foreign subsidiaries. There is more convergence in recent data, however, and the UN now estimates cumulative inflows of $47bn between 1989 and 1996 for the whole region.

Table 2.8 sets out the UN data for the CEE-10 from 1990 to 1996. Owing to a surge in inflows in 1996, Poland has received nearly one-third of investment inflows followed by Hungary, the Czech Republic and then Russia. Hungary's inflows are particularly large relative to its size, while inflows into Russia are small. These four countries take around 80% of all FDI into the region, showing the concentration of flows on a

Table 2.8: Cumulative FDI inflows to CEE and CIS, 1990–96[a]

	Cumulative flows (US$m)	% of total flows	Inflows per capita (US$)
Poland	13,503	28.7	350.73
Hungary	12,936	27.5	1,255.92
Czech Republic[b]	6,938	14.8	673.61
Romania	1,595	3.4	70.26
Slovakia[b]	1,007	2.1	189.96
Estonia	799	1.7	532.67
Latvia	760	1.6	304.00
Slovenia	688	1.5	344.00
Bulgaria	502	1.1	59.76
Lithuania	296	0.6	80.00
CEE-10 total	39,024	83.0	370.95
Russian Federation	4,054	8.6	27.34
Other CIS and CEE countries[c]	3,949	8.4	26.83
Total flows to CEE and CIS	47,027	100.0	117.36

[a] 1996 figures are UN estimates.
[b] Own calculation made of allocation of FDI inflows to Czechoslovakia prior to 1993.
[c] Includes the other CIS countries and Albania.
Source: own calculations based on UN (1997) and World Bank (1996).

few destinations. While market size is one important determinant of FDI flows, success in political and economic transition is also a key factor (Estrin et al. 1997). Thus, success breeds success; stable, successful transition attracts FDI, which further contributes to transition. Moreover, investors show the same preferences as the EU and NATO in terms of the countries' relative progress.

Table 2.9 sets out a more detailed picture of investment inflows across the CEE countries. The absence of data in the early years reflects a mixture of low investment and data problems. Hungary's success in maintaining high investment flows is clear, although its receipts dropped somewhat in 1996. An initial drop in investment flows subsequent to the Czechoslovakian split was reversed in 1994 and the Czech Republic saw a large increase in 1995. Inflows into Poland, which had been relatively low, given its size, picked up from 1993 onwards and surged in 1996. A more modest increase in inflows is also seen in a number of other countries, and the total for the region in 1995 was more than double that

Table 2.9: Inflows of FDI to CEE, Russia and Ukraine, 1990–96 ($m)

	1990	*1991*	*1992*	*1993*	*1994*	*1995*	*1996[a]*
Bulgaria	4	56	42	55	105	90	150
Czech Republic	–	–	–	654	878	2,568	1,200
Former Czechoslovakia	207	600	1,103	–	–	–	–
Estonia	–	–	82	162	215	202	138
Hungary	–	1,462	1,479	2,350	1,144	4,519	1,982
Latvia	–	–	29	45	214	180	292
Lithuania	–	–	10	30	31	73	152
Poland	89	291	678	1,715	1,875	3,659	5,196
Romania	–	40	77	94	341	419	624
Slovakia	–	–	–	199	203	183	150
Slovenia	–	–	111	113	128	176	160
Total CEE–10	300	2,449	3,611	5,417	5,134	12,069	10,044
Russian Federation	–	–	700	700	637	2,017	1,800
Ukraine	–	–	200	200	159	267	440

[a] UN estimates.
Source: UN (1997).

for 1994. Flows in 1996 were lower than in 1995 but still double the 1994 level, with cumulative flows for 1990–96 of just under $40bn. Early estimates for 1997 by the EBRD (1997) suggest FDI jumped again by around $18bn, of which almost half went to Poland and Russia. In 1996 investment flows into Poland moved ahead of those into Hungary, although Hungarian per capita flows remained higher.

The Western source countries for FDI into CEE vary (Table 2.10). Germany and the United States dominate with about 20% of total investment each (Estrin et al. 1997); France has about 7% and the UK about 4%. As with the trade data, the FDI data reinforce the picture of unevenness in EU–CEE integration, with Germany playing a particularly important role and the UK, notably, a much smaller role relative to their respective shares of international trade and investment (see Grabbe 1997). However, there is considerable variation in Germany's shares of FDI across the countries and overall Germany is not as dominant as in the trade flows. Shares of FDI are thus fairly similar to relative shares of trade among the EU member states, although there is considerable variation by year because of the effect that large single investments have on the total.

Table 2.10: Total FDI by source country for the Czech Republic, Hungary[a] and Poland, 1990–95

	Cumulative 1990–95[b]	
	$m	%
USA	3,472.4	22.6
Germany	3,222.9	21.0
Netherlands	1,435.9	9.3
Switzerland[c]	1,122.2	7.3
France	1,095.6	7.1
Austria	1,012.8	6.6
UK[d]	700.3	4.5
Italy[e]	472.1	3.0
Other	2,771.0	18.1
Total	15,305.2	100.0

[a] Hungary total excludes greenfield.
[b] Czech data to March 1996; Hungary to October 1995; Poland to September 1995.
[c] No data available for Swiss investment in Hungary.
[d] No data available for British investment in Czech Republic.
[e] No data available for Italian investment in Hungary; Czech data only to 1994.
Source: Estrin, Hughes and Todd (1997).

A number of commentators and analysts have expressed disappointment and concern at the low levels of foreign direct investment into CEE (World Bank 1996, Baldwin 1994), but it is not clear that the data support this conclusion (see Estrin et al. 1997). FDI flows were low initially, but this is inevitable given the risks and uncertainties of transition and the need to develop appropriate legal and institutional frameworks and market structures. Subsequently, FDI growth rates have been very high indeed and per capita levels into the top three CEE countries compare well with those into a number of EU member states and also with flows into some of the main developing-country recipients of FDI (Estrin et al. 1997). Hungarian FDI per head places it just after France, Spain and the UK (the biggest EU recipients) and ahead of Portugal. On a per capita basis, flows into the three leading CEE countries are substantially higher than those into the leading host developing countries, although in absolute terms these countries mostly (though not all) receive more (Estrin et al. 1997).

It is clear, however, that FDI flows into CEE have been concentrated on a small number of countries. Important factors here include success in

23

economic and political transition, market size, labour costs, location and government policy (Estrin et al. 1997). While market size is important and differs across countries, the importance of success in transition suggests that other countries will begin to attract substantially more FDI as they proceed with economic development. Overall, it is unclear how important accession to the EU will be in affecting future investment flows. Given that flows are high in Hungary, the Czech Republic and Poland, substantial investment both for market and labour cost reasons is likely to continue to occur prior to EU accession. Expectations of future EU membership may influence investment (as happened with previous enlargements of the EU), but flows also tend to correlate with success in economic and political transition. The high rates of increase in FDI anticipated by some (for example Baldwin et al. 1997) after EU accession may not occur if substantial investment flows are actually experienced beforehand.

Future trends in integration

EU–CEE economic integration seems likely to continue its rapid pace, given the high levels of trade growth since 1989 and the increasing attraction of FDI into CEE discussed in this section. Estimates of the potential for future growth in EU–CEE trade range widely and are based on a variety of approaches and models (see Collins and Rodrik 1991, Wang and Winters 1991, Hamilton and Winters 1992, Hughes and Hare 1992, Baldwin 1994, Brown et al. 1997, Neven 1995). Overall, trade seems likely at least to double in the medium term (Hamilton and Winters 1992, Baldwin 1994, CEC 1994, Baldwin 1995, Cadot et al. 1995). In the long term, it could rise at least several times more (Neven 1995) if potential dynamic gains from rapid transfer of technology and managerial skills are realized and a virtuous circle of trade expansion and faster growth develops. Much will depend on the path of economic transition in CEE and other factors, such as exchange rate policy and trends in foreign investment. In addition, there are marked differences between the CEE countries as potential markets.

The CEE countries are already gaining many benefits from economic integration before actually becoming members of the EU. In addition to gaining foreign investment and preferential access to EU markets and enjoying increased competition, they are being locked into a framework for economic liberalization and adjustment to EU norms through the pre-accession strategy which itself fosters economic integration. Integration may also have had some costs, such as overly rapid market-opening and a possibly artificial bias towards EU markets rather than intra-CEE integration (Drábek and Smith 1995). Attempting to follow EU policy models may also have costs if other institutional structures are more appropriate. Furthermore, undergoing a process of transition to a market economy at the same time as orienting trade towards the EU may make CEE countries particularly subject to the influence of EU integration in encouraging the development of some sectors and the decline of others.

The economic impact of enlargement

Once accession actually takes place, how much difference will it make to integration? For the CEE countries, there could be significant benefits in several areas. The first is that accession would also give the CEE countries a say in EU decision-making. This issue was central to EFTA members' motivations for joining the EU. Secondly, there are several blocked areas which are unlikely to see much progress before accession. Particularly important are the liberalization of trade in agricultural goods and the lifting of contingent protection provisions, both of which would occur once CEE countries were full members.

The third area is access to the Single Market, which is generally expected to give a considerable boost to CEE exporters, as well as further stabilizing CEE economic policy. The likely effect is difficult to assess because of the lack of consensus about the impact of the Single Market Programme on the EU-12 countries, particularly because of the need to take into account dynamic effects and scale effects. Moreover, the timetable for extension of the Single Market is uncertain, and there are likely to be transitional periods, derogations and extension of only some of the four freedoms to begin with.

The Single Market seems likely to have a lesser effect on CEE economic development than it did on the EU-12, whose trade had already reached a steady state by the mid-1980s; nevertheless, additional trade as a result of access to the Single Market may have a relatively small impact on the CEE countries in comparison with the strong effects of general opening of trade since 1989. What needs much more analysis (as discussed in Chapter 5) is the economic impact on CEE of taking on the Single Market *acquis* (the body of EU legislation governing it).

For the EU, the economic impact of enlargement is likely to be smaller, given the small size of the CEE economies. Studies published by CEPR (CEPR 1990, Baldwin 1994, contributions to Faini and Portes 1995, Winters 1995, Baldwin et al. 1997) and others (for example Brown et al. 1997) suggest that the aggregate impact will be small and mostly positive. The most recent estimates (Baldwin et al. 1997) suggest an overall gain for the EU-15 of about 10bn ECU in real income. However, Baldwin et al. find that these gains are likely to be very unevenly distributed across the EU countries, with Germany, France and the United Kingdom together getting 70% of the total gain. The trade data presented above suggest that beyond the three main traders (Germany, Austria and Italy) there is currently a relative lack of economic interest in the CEE countries in comparison with interests in the EU and third countries. Whether this interest will increase depends on whether the rest of the EU can catch up with Germany's level of integration.

Some authors (e.g. Baldwin 1994) have argued that the potential for catch-up by the rest of the EU is high, given medium-run trade potential relative to existing levels (see Baldwin 1994, Vittas and Mauro 1997). However, it is questionable to assume that Germany's trade and investment levels will reach a steady state. Germany has already pulled further ahead of the rest of the EU (see Table 2.4 above), and German exporters could continue to build on any first-mover advantage in terms of market knowledge, brand-building and FDI to increase their market share.

With regard to the sectoral distribution of gains and losses, there is little firm evidence yet of any clear patterns. Looking at potential sectoral and regional effects, Faini and Portes (1995) conclude from a number of studies that the impact of rapid import growth would be negligible and that trade with southern Europe is likely to be mostly intra-industry, with few distributional implications. They and other authors (Rollo and Smith 1993, Dittus and Andersen 1995) argue that even sensitive sectors are unlikely to suffer large adjustment costs. Wyplosz (1995) concludes that, although there are strong effects on wages and employment in specific industries, the results are not systematic across industries and countries. Particularly important in the impact of enlargement on specific industrial sectors could be the likelihood of a high proportion of intra-industry trade, which would lower transitional costs (see Faini and Portes 1995, Drábek and Smith 1995). However, meaningful analysis of this issue would require considerably deeper investigation of the commodity composition of EU–CEE trade than has so far been undertaken.

Implications for competitiveness

Economic integration with CEE countries could affect the competitiveness of west European industries if the region proves to be an area of dynamic growth and low production costs. The region could cause structural changes in west European industry if cheaper CEE inputs and market opportunities for EU firms to expand in the CEE countries increase the competitiveness of the parts of western Europe most integrated with CEE relative to the rest of the region (Hughes 1996).

Overall, the continued importance of German firms in CEE markets could cause the German economy to benefit most among EU countries from the potential structural changes in west European industry that result from integration with CEE economies. German industry could see some activities continuing to relocate to and expand in CEE locations, and a general refocusing on higher-value-added activities. Such an outcome would increase Germany's competitiveness relative to the rest of the EU. Given recent concerns about German competitiveness, this is to be welcomed, but rapid changes in relative economic performance across the EU could cause tensions, particularly in the context of EMU.

The success with which the EU is able to deal with the restructuring implied by integration with CEE has important implications for the politics of EU–CEE relations, but it may not have direct political effects on the process of enlargement. In the years preceding the first accessions (assuming these take place in the first decade of the next century), these economic effects may not be obvious or large, and economic interests in CEE will not necessarily drive enlargement policies in any case. There is a much more complex set of political and security considerations lying behind EU member states' enlargement policies, as well as the complex calculations of the effects of enlargement on the EU budget.

Conclusions

Economic integration with CEE is already occurring even before enlargement of the EU. The development of new market economies has led to increased trade flows in both directions and to rising inflows of FDI to the CEE countries. Integration is influenced to some extent by the prospect of accession in that CEE countries' adherence to the policy framework of the EU's pre-accession strategy is changing those countries' institutional framework and policies and locking them into a process of adaptation to EU norms. The major questions are how EU integration will affect the CEE countries' competitiveness in the longer term, and whether most of the economic benefits of integration will be realized before accession. More difficult to assess are the long-term economic benefits of the contribution that enlargement is likely to make to the creation of a more stable and secure Europe (the 'peace dividend'), but this factor also needs to be taken into account when considering its overall economic impact.

The data on economic integration presented in this chapter indicate that major negative effects from increasing trade are unlikely, while positive effects are not negligible and are likely to increase; indeed, for some EU members CEE trade is already starting to assume a significant role in total trade. There are already notable differences between EU members' interests in CEE as a whole and between the CEE countries in their attractiveness as additions to the EU. Germany's strong geo-political interests in CEE are being reinforced by its dominance of EU trade and FDI flows, and some other countries have substantial economic interests in CEE. Although they have small shares of total EU trade with CEE, Austria, Greece and Finland conduct a significant share of their extra-EU trade with the region. However, the effects of integration may be weaker for other parts of the EU economy, and current economic interests are small for countries such as Portugal, Ireland, the UK and Spain.

The fact that overall EU economic interests in the CEE countries are at present fairly small (even if they have considerable potential to grow in the long term), combined with the likelihood that many of the economic benefits of integration through trade and investment will be realized prior to accession, could mean that the significance of eventual membership will lie more in its political and security benefits than in economic ones for both the EU and the CEE applicants. The economic issues are likely to remain more significant for the CEE countries – guaranteeing market access, opening agricultural markets, and, not least, the overall impact of adopting the Single Market *acquis*.

In the political economy of enlargement, fear of adverse effects in particular regions and sectors has strong political resonance, even if these turn out to be unfounded and the aggregate effect is minuscule. It is not yet clear whether particular interest groups will expect losses owing to CEE competition and, if they do, whether they will be able to mobilize support in a way that slows down the process of enlargement. However, as with the budgetary politics of enlargement, the key to the process is whether or not EU member states move towards an agreement that allows the overall calculation of economic, political and security interests in enlargement to override any fears of geographically or sectorally con- centrated losses.

Chapter 3

Progress so far: the pre-accession strategy

Introduction

In the first years after 1989 the EU was slow to respond to the changes in CEE, with member states showing reluctance to commit themselves to eastward enlargement even in principle. The EU has since developed a series of institutional structures and policy approaches which together represent a significant commitment to enlargement, but the likely timing and extent of the process remain unclear. Overall, it is questionable whether the EU has a coherent strategy for enlargement, in terms of a comprehensive analysis of what a 26-member-state Union would be like – its institutions, functioning and policies – as well as the path to achieving this goal. The reasons for this lack of clear strategy lie in the different views between and within member states about how the EU should develop in the future, including the preferred speed and extent of enlargement, which have implications for institutional and policy changes. In developing the EU's pre-accession strategy, the European Commission has had to work within these political constraints.

The pre-accession strategy has been criticized for being developed relatively slowly, for focusing on criteria for the CEE countries rather than on necessary changes on the EU side, and for not setting out a clear timetable or sequence of priorities or milestones (see e.g. Inotai 1995). Given the lack of overall strategic vision from member states, it is inevitable that the EU's approach is somewhat technical and *ad hoc*. None the less, the various agreements established between the CEE countries and the EU cumulatively represent a strong overall commitment to enlargement and some detailed processes for moving towards negotiations.

This chapter covers the development of the pre-accession strategy so far and assesses its main features. Chapters 4, 5 and 6 then analyse the European Commission's proposals for reinforcing the strategy and for reforming the EU to cope with enlargement, presented in July 1997 in 'Agenda 2000'.

Development of the pre-accession strategy

The original strategy was formally launched at the Essen European Council in December 1994, but it incorporates earlier agreements and commitments. Its main purpose is to guide applicants towards fulfilling the main conditions for membership set out at the Copenhagen European Council. The accession conditions set at Copenhagen in 1993 are as follows:

> Membership requires that the candidate country has achieved stability of institutions guaranteeing democracy, the rule of law, human rights and respect for and protection of minorities, the existence of a functioning market economy as well as the capacity to cope with competitive pressure and market forces within the Union. Membership presupposes the candidate's ability to take on the obligations of membership including adherence to the aims of political, economic and monetary union. (European Council 1993)

The Copenhagen summit results were an important commitment to enlargement by the EU, but the three main conditions for membership are extremely broad, and provide neither clear criteria for accession nor a timetable. Moreover, no new entrant has ever taken on the full *acquis* on accession, so the ability to 'take on the obligations of membership' is open to interpretation (see Chapter 5).

In addition to these conditions for applicants, the European Council stated that 'The Union's capacity to absorb new members, while maintaining the momentum of European Integration, is also an important consideration in the general interest of both the Union and the candidate countries.' This is an indication of concerns that enlargement might threaten the EU's functioning, particularly if institutional and policy reforms were inadequate or progress towards EMU faltered. At the Amsterdam summit in June 1997, EU leaders decided that the very limited institutional reforms they had agreed would be sufficient until the number of member states exceeded 20, so putting off the particularly controversial issues of voting in the Council and the relations between the three pillars of the Union (European Community, Common Foreign and Security Policy, and Justice and Home Affairs). Other questions about the functioning of an enlarged EU remain, most notably the new budget to run from 2000 and whether EMU stays on track (see Chapter 7).

The Essen summit established the pre-accession strategy by extending the Europe Agreements to the Baltic states and Slovenia, establishing the multilateral Structured Dialogue and calling for the preparation of a White Paper on the Single Market. The Madrid summit in December 1995 reaffirmed the commitment to enlargement, calling on the Commission to prepare *avis* on the CEE applications for membership to be ready shortly after the conclusion of the 1996 Intergovernmental Conference (IGC), and expressed the hope that negotiations would start at the same time as those with Cyprus and Malta, which were due six months after the conclusion of the IGC.[1]

The Amsterdam summit in June 1997 reaffirmed the EU's commitment to opening negotiations with Cyprus and at least some of the CEE applicants. However, in shying away from decisions on key areas of institutional reform, particularly voting procedures, at the conclusion of the IGC, the EU has extended the time scale of its own process of preparing for enlargement and has postponed dealing with the issues raised by its commitment to eventually incorporating another 11 member states.

The key elements

The four main elements of the pre-accession strategy until the publication of Agenda 2000 were the Europe Agreements, the Single Market White Paper, the Phare programme and the Structured Dialogue. The first two elements set a general framework for adapting to EU requirements, while the last two were intended to facilitate this process. They began at different times and vary in their purpose and legal status, but all four elements are intended to guide applicants in their preparations for membership.

The Europe Agreements
The Europe Agreements need not be a precursor to accession; they can exist as a set of formally structured trade relations in their own right, and they provide a general framework for political and economic cooperation. The Agreements were signed bilaterally with each CEE country from 1993 onwards,[2] and are intended to 'establish a free trade area in a

[1] Malta subsequently froze its application.
[2] Owing to the delay in implementation because of the need for ratification of mixed agreements, Interim Agreements put into effect the trade provisions before the Europe Agreements came into force.

Progress so far: the pre-accession strategy

transitional period lasting a maximum of 10 years'[3] from their entry into force, on an asymmetric basis and in two stages. Various deadlines for EU market-opening were brought forward at the 1993 European Council in Copenhagen following criticism of the long timetable. Duties and quantitative restrictions were removed on over half of the total exports of the Visegrad countries (the Czech Republic, Hungary, Poland and Slovakia) immediately the Europe Agreements came into effect. This percentage rose to 60% by January 1993 and is expected to reach 85% by the beginning of 1998 (CEC 1995). The remaining 15% of total exports still subject to restrictions is expected to be composed of agricultural products.

The academic literature has seen considerable discussion about the policy framework for trade and investment and its likely effects on trade flows. The initial focus of debate was on whether the remaining restrictions on trade were justified by the likely economic effects of greater market-opening by the EU, with the particular criticism that the EU could have been more generous in the market access it granted to CEE exports of sensitive products (Hamilton and Winters 1992, Messerlin 1992, Rollo and Smith 1993, Drábek and Smith 1995). Most of the quotas, tariffs and other restrictions on sensitive industrial goods have since been lifted, but agricultural products are still subject to a complex regime based on levy or tariff quota concessions. This situation makes agricultural trade a sensitive issue in EU–CEE relations, and a significant further liberalization of trade in agriculture seems unlikely before a substantial reform of the CAP and the start of enlargement negotiations.

There are still wide-ranging contingent protection provisions, whose effects are a subject of debate (EBRD 1994, Winters 1995b, Nuti 1997). The agreements leave considerable scope for protectionist measures to be reintroduced within the current framework, and anti-dumping and countervailing duty actions may remain a deterrent to exporters (EBRD 1994, Drábek and Smith 1995). Although the number of actions so far taken against associated countries is relatively small, the threat of them may have had inhibiting effects on business decisions.

At a more specific level, the rules of origin caused initial controversy because the Europe Agreements did not permit cumulation of local content between the Visegrad countries and others (see EBRD 1994). Such rules have the potential to discourage intra-CEE trade because there are lower tariffs on imports from the EU than on those from other CEE

[3] Article 7 in Hungary's Europe Agreement.

32

countries (Baldwin 1994). Progress seems to have been made in this area since the Essen European Council, which made a commitment to a multilateral cumulation of origin rules, and an agreement with CEE was expected to be put into effect in 1997.

Recent literature has shown more emphasis on the implications of the policy framework for the development of trade institutions and laws, particularly in the CEE countries (see Winters 1995a). In addition to affecting economic integration in Europe, this aspect of the policy framework has implications for transition in CEE by its impact on policy formation and institutional development. An important aspect of the Europe Agreement framework is that it can tie the CEE countries into trade liberalization and counter domestic pressure for protection (Sapir 1995). On the CEE side, initially rapid trade liberalization was followed by a partial reintroduction of import protection in some CEE countries in 1991–2 in response to the output shock and the collapse of the CMEA (see EBRD 1994, Messerlin 1995). According to Sapir (1995), looking at the case of Hungary, protection was reintroduced in areas where the Europe Agreement imposes little discipline, suggesting that the Europe Agreement is partly responsible for maintaining liberalization in CEE trade policy.

Overall, the Europe Agreements have been beneficial to CEE–EU trade in offering some advances on the trade concessions made under the multilateral Generalized System of Preferences, and they continue to provide a stable framework for trade relations. In view of the small economic effects of giving trade preferences to the CEE countries, the EU could have afforded to be more generous in its provisions and faster in liberalizing trade (Faini and Portes 1995, Winters 1995a, Inotai 1995). In CEE, the initially controversial elements of the Europe Agreements seem to have lost salience now that most of the restrictions on trade in industrial goods have been lifted, although a strong feeling lingers that the EU could have been considerably more generous on access for agricultural goods. In the two countries that have had the most trade disputes with the EU, Poland and the Czech Republic, there are still concerns that their economies have been opened too fast, but options for dealing with balance-of-payments problems are constrained by the Europe Agreements.

Given the size of the 'development gap' with central and eastern Europe (discussed in Inotai 1994) and the scale of the changes that the CEE countries have been making since 1989, greater help from western Europe might have been expected in terms of market access. The major remaining issues are agriculture and contingent protection, on which substantial progress seems unlikely in advance of formal negotiations for accession. These are areas where formal accession to the EU, rather than just upgraded trade relations, would make a significant difference to furthering trade liberalization and economic integration. For those CEE countries excluded from the first wave of accessions, on the other hand, offers of greater access for agricultural products would be an important way of encouraging further integration with the EU.

The Single Market White Paper

Prepared by the Commission and then endorsed by the European Council in June 1995, the Single Market White Paper is intended to set out the key legislation governing trade in goods and services in the EU's Internal Market. In each sector it divides the legislation into 'Stage 1' measures, which set out the basic policies essential to the functioning of the Single Market and the instruments required to implement them, and then the 'Stage 2' detailed implementing rules. However, the White Paper does not provide an overall prioritization between sectors, although suggestions are made about sequencing; countries have had to make their own distinctions between measures that are required simply for accession and those that are also of immediate benefit to countries in transition, and this has complicated strategies for integration (see World Bank 1997, Preston 1997). The onus is on the applicant countries to decide on priorities and speed, drawing up their own national programmes and timetables for implementation; this means that they have had to make considerable commitments to the process of alignment without an indication from the EU of how much progress is necessary to start negotiations. Moreover, the White Paper provides no reciprocal commitments on the part of the EU, despite the obligations imposed on the applicants (Smith et al. 1996). CEE government administrations are in a weak bargaining position and have simply had to accept the White Paper's demands owing to their status as applicants, which gives them very little political room for manoeuvre in relations with the EU.

Even though it has no legal force (unlike the Europe Agreements), the White Paper has been very influential in guiding the preparations of applicants towards global membership. However, the main focus of their efforts so far has been legislative approximation, primarily at the formal level of writing EU directives into national law. There has been some surprise on the EU side at the speed with which some countries have progressed in translating and incorporating the Single Market legislation, but there are doubts about the extent of their progress in actually implementing it, as the Commission acknowledges in its *avis* published in Agenda 2000.

Despite the emphasis in the White Paper on setting up the institutional framework for monitoring and enforcement, this side of the process still requires many more years of work in all of the CEE countries, and the devotion of considerably more resources. Even for the applicants that have made most progress in approximation, moving from the formal establishment of Single Market legislation to its implementation, which will involve setting up everything from standards and certification bodies to new emergency telephone numbers, poses major challenges to national administration capabilities.

Civil servants in all countries have experienced major problems with taking on the administrative burdens imposed by the White Paper, and there seem to have been a number of debates within ministries about how to approximate regulations and how to prioritize between sectors (see Preston 1997, World Bank 1997). It is hardly surprising that adoption of the *acquis* is proving so problematic. The CEE countries are taking on a far more complex body of legislation than did previous applicants, owing to the Single Market, moves towards EMU and the development of the second and third pillars, and the applicants are starting with much more rudimentary institutional frameworks at national level. Not only does this stretch the legal and technical capacity of the applicants, but they also have to develop processes to respond to EU demands during a period of major systemic change (Preston 1997), and they also have to adopt the *acquis* much more quickly than previous applicants, who had Association Agreements with long time scales or 20 years of adjustment through EFTA.

The Single Market White Paper aided this process by providing a substantive document and a set of areas on which to work. It was an explicit recognition that the Single Market had become the core of the *acquis*. However, it leaves a number of unanswered questions. It does not cover the full *acquis*, but as yet there is no similar guidance for the areas left out, notably agriculture, the environment, energy, transport and social policy. A central issue for political decision as well as technical assessment is how much of the *acquis* the applicant countries have to take on before accession and how much afterwards. Greece, Portugal and Spain gained very long transitional periods in some areas; in Agenda 2000 the European Commission has argued against any form of derogation for the CEE countries, but this leaves open the question of the scope and duration of transitional periods that might be negotiated. There are concerns among member states that transitional periods should not threaten the integrity of the Single Market, and among applicants that they should ensure full access to it by avoiding requests for transitions. However, both sides face sensitive issues in negotiations where they will be under pressure to agree to transitional periods (see Chapter 5).

There is also the question of whether full implementation of the four freedoms (goods, services, capital and labour) is necessary on accession. It has been argued that a swifter enlargement could be achieved by allowing the CEE economies substantial derogations in terms of production conditions (environmental and social standards, for example) while insisting that the products themselves meet Single Market standards (see Smith et al. 1996). However, an early and general concession of this type might reduce pressure that would otherwise lead successfully to adjustments and change of standards. Furthermore, it is unclear to what extent the different CEE countries face serious difficulties in meeting most production conditions, at least on the social side (see Chapter 4).

This issue is politically sensitive for both sides because it relates to the speed with which CEE countries could be integrated into the Single Market and their competitiveness within it. Member states are unlikely to agree to substantial or long transitional periods for meeting EU standards if CEE firms are to have full access to their markets; indeed, there have already been allegations of social and environmental 'dumping' by CEE firms meeting lower standards than their EU counterparts. Thus, member states are unlikely to be receptive to proposals for any sort of general concession on process or product standards.

At present it is uncertain how far businesses are actually adopting Single Market standards or governments are able to monitor and enforce EU legislation. Moreover, there is still great uncertainty about the potential costs to business and the implications of taking on Single Market legislation (see EBRD 1995, 1997), and Agenda 2000 provides no further information on this question. Given that EU legislation seems to have had a considerable influence in guiding reforms in a range of policy areas, particularly where there was little or no previous regulation, this question merits considerably more attention.

In addition to the question of how much the whole process might cost, it is debatable whether the intense process of legislative alignment provoked by the White Paper is appropriate for all the applicants' circumstances. There is clearly an opportunity cost to the resource-intensive preparations for alignment with Single Market norms, and this could be great for CEE administrations which face severe administrative and financial constraints. Although the overall goal of integrating CEE economies into the Single Market is generally accepted as beneficial to their overall development, the White Paper approach places heavy administrative burdens on countries with little spare capacity, potentially diverting attention and resources from more basic and immediate needs. The general purpose of economic integration with the EU is broadly expected to lead to greater trade and investment opportunities, but meeting the demands of the pre-accession strategy at this stage in transition may not have that effect unless candidates gain interim benefits as well as the prospect of accession, such as improving their access to EU markets beyond the Europe Agreements. At the moment, however, further liberalization looks unlikely until accession itself.

This issue is particularly relevant in the case of the countries furthest back in the queue, which might not join for over a decade and are having the greatest problems with transition. There is clearly an overlap between basic development needs and Single Market requirements in areas such as competition policy, where many post-communist economies had no existing legislation, but there is often a conflict for resources. For the lagging applicants who might not join for many years, concentrating on adaptation to the complex regimes governing EU-wide traffic in goods and services may be particularly inappropriate in the context of much more pressing needs. Moreover, in some areas there are also arguably more appropriate models for countries in transition than EU ones, such as US or developing-country systems, so complying with EU demands may have opportunity costs here too. After all, the Single Market legislation was developed for economies at a very different stage of development, and it contains anomalies and complications arising from the political context of the member state preferences in which it was framed. Although applicants will ultimately have to accept and comply with the rules of the club they want to join, the sequencing of preparations could be much more closely aligned with the development needs of applicants. For example, the White Paper has been criticized for not distinguishing between measures that may be intrinsically important for transition and those that are necessary primarily in order to join the Single Market (Smith et al. 1996).

The Phare programme

Phare was established in 1990 to provide aid and technical assistance to support the process of economic restructuring and transition more generally; it became part of the pre-accession strategy under the logic that it would aid the process of integration. Phare was progressively extended to cover all ten of the applicants for membership, together with Albania, Bosnia-Herzegovina and the former Yugoslav Republic of Macedonia. (Croatia's participation is currently suspended.) The programme's overall results are difficult to assess, as it has covered a wide range of projects in different countries, sometimes complementing and occasionally competing with other bilateral or multilateral aid and assistance. It is clear that a substantial proportion of Phare funds has flowed back to the West to pay for consultancy advice (Court of Auditors 1997). The efficacy and appropriateness of the enormous range of advice received is open to debate, but overall there is likely to be less need for such a preponderance of consultancy as economic and political transition progresses.

There have been problems with Phare's operations owing to administrative problems at EU level and in the CEE countries. Particular problems with delivery of programmes in several recipient countries are part of the explanation for the differing amounts received per capita across CEE (see Table 3.1). In various of its *avis*, the Commission points to funds being left unused because of lack of compliance with conditionality (Slovakia) and administrative bottlenecks (Slovakia and Bulgaria). In the CEE countries there is criticism of the overall functioning of the programme, particularly the fact that it is overly bureaucratic and inflexible. These problems on both sides will clearly have to be dealt with if the further funds which the EU is preparing to extend to CEE prior to and after accession are to be used effectively.

The Structured Dialogue
The final element in the original pre-accession strategy was the Structured Dialogue. It was intended as a forum for multilateral discussion of issues, a welcome departure from the preponderance of bilateral agreements with CEE; however, it lacked decision-making powers and any clear focus. As a result, what was sometimes referred to as 'the unstructured monologue' tended to be given relatively little attention by Western politicians. CEE politicians and policy-makers have evaluated it as primarily a talking-shop and a token commitment while the EU stalled on any more serious initiatives. The Structured Dialogue is acknowledged to have had some utility in the process of resolving the disputes between Slovenia and Italy, but frequent comments on the multilateral meetings are that few EU members attended and that, although it fostered

Table 3.1: Phare receipts, 1990–96

	Total receipts (approx.), (m ECU)	ECU per capita
Bulgaria[a]	476	57
Czech Republic	433	42
Estonia[b]	120	80
Hungary	673	66
Latvia[b]	124	50
Lithuania[b]	179	48
Poland	1,400	36
Romania	731	32
Slovakia[c]	212	39
Slovenia	94	47

[a] Bulgaria was allocated no new funding in 1996 because of unused funds from previous years.
[b] Total for 1992–6 only. The Baltic states did not receive Phare funds prior to independence from the Soviet Union, although they received some assistance through TACIS.
[c] Slovakia was allocated no new funding in 1996.
Source: CEC *avis* and own calculations.

contact, its discussions were only symbolic as its lack of decision-making powers made it insubstantial.

There is widespread (if not official) agreement among policy-makers in the EU as well that the Structured Dialogue has been relatively ineffective. The Commission has recommended in Agenda 2000 that it be abandoned, to be replaced partly by bilateral meetings and *ad hoc* multilateral ones; however, concern has since been expressed at the prospect of having no multilateral forum for discussion of issues affecting both applicants and member states. There is thus a clear need for a more substantial body to play this role effectively, and it is unclear to what extent the proposed European Conference would do so (see Chapter 5).

Conclusion

Until the end of the IGC and publication of Agenda 2000, the EU's pre-accession strategy was focused primarily on technical issues of alignment by the applicants and on *ad hoc* preparations on the EU side. The Europe Agreements and the Single Market White Paper set a framework for relations and substantive guidelines for applicants in their preparations, but there is a consensus among policy-makers that the strategy now needs strengthening. Moreover, the strategy focused only on adjustment and development in the applicant countries and not on the EU side, and it failed to provide a strategic assessment of what an enlarged EU might look like.

On the CEE side, the process of simultaneous political and economic transitions poses post-communist countries with much greater challenges than those encountered by previous applicants. In setting conditions for membership, the EU has to find a balance between giving support to reforming governments while not devaluing the status of EU membership by admitting countries that fail to meet its standards. In developing a strategy for guiding efforts towards fulfilling these conditions, the EU needs to ensure its relevance to countries in transition; in this context there are already questions about the EU's generosity towards applicants and potential conflict between their needs in transition and the detailed requirements of EU membership.

In Agenda 2000, the European Commission has now outlined a reinforced pre-accession strategy, along with a set of proposals for preparing the EU for enlargement through budgetary and policy reform. The next two chapters consider the Commission's *avis* on the applications and the next steps in enlargement, including the issues surrounding opening negotiations and the proposals for reinforcing the pre-accession strategy.

Chapter 4

Readiness for membership and the Commission's avis

Introduction

The process of simultaneous political and economic transitions poses the post-communist CEE countries with much greater challenges than those encountered by previous applicants. Not only do they have much more to do in establishing market economies and democratic political systems, but the EU is considerably more integrated than at the time of previous enlargements and is becoming more so. The EU established its pre-accession strategy in recognition of the particular challenge the CEE applicants face, but it has also set additional and more general criteria for accession under the Copenhagen conditions; these conditions cover political and economic transition, as well as the ability to take on the obligations of membership (see Chapter 3).

The general democracy and market economy conditions are very broad, and it is unclear how much progress in the various areas has to be made prior to accession, although the *avis* now show to a large extent how the Commission interprets these criteria. The third condition about taking on the obligations of membership is the traditional one facing countries wishing to accede to the EU, and the *avis* also give the Commission's view on their progress. Meeting these conditions represents a major challenge for economies and societies in transition, and their progress in achieving explicit and implicit conditions is open to debate.

This chapter considers the European Commission's *avis* on the ten applicants set out in Agenda 2000 (CEC 1997) in July 1997 and the issues involved in their post-communist political and economic transitions. In Chapter 5 we consider the issues involved in negotiations and the

Commission's proposals for reinforcing the pre-accession strategy in Agenda 2000.

Meeting the Copenhagen conditions

The Commission's *avis* on the ten applications of the CEE countries are unique in the history of EU enlargements in that they do not merely judge applicants' readiness for membership now, but rather take a medium-term view on whether they will be able to meet the conditions for membership within the timespan of negotiations. The *avis* thus give an overview of the political and economic situations in the ten countries up to May 1997 and also an assessment of how close they might come to being ready to join in five years' time. This inevitably introduces an element of speculation, and leaves room for applicants who are not recommended to start negotiations to argue that they could make faster progress than the Commission expects and so should move into negotiations at the start.

In the ten *avis* published as part of Agenda 2000 in July 1997, the Commission does not set out the sources of information used in its analysis and assessments. It is known that, in addition to the lengthy replies received from the applicants to its own questionnaire, it has considered a range of sources of expertise beyond the Commission, including analyses by other international institutions, and inputs from experts, academics and various parts of the policy-making community. However, it is impossible to tell from the *avis* the relative weight or importance ascribed to different sources.

The Commission's overall recommendation is that negotiations should start with five countries: the Czech Republic, Estonia, Hungary, Poland and Slovenia. It recommends that Latvia, Lithuania, Romania and Bulgaria be excluded on economic grounds, although their problems are assessed as being of different orders of severity. Slovakia is the only country that is judged to have failed to meet the political conditions, although its economy is assessed relatively favourably. Apart from these recommendations, the Commission does not explicitly rank the ten applicants, but the *avis* are written in such a way as to make direct comparison straightforward (as is discussed further below).

Application of the additional Copenhagen political and economic conditions did not lead the Commission to a markedly different ranking of countries than the one resulting from its assessment of their ability to take on the *acquis*, except in the case of Slovakia, where the failure to meet the democracy condition was the critical factor. The Luxembourg

European Council in December 1997 decided the member states' response to the Commission's recommendations and, in particular, with whom to open negotiations. Negotiations will begin under the British presidency of the EU in the first half of 1998.

The nature of transition

The wave of political revolutions across CEE from 1989 onwards has caused regime changes of an unprecedented nature. Abandoning central planning and its concomitant political controls at such speed has required far-reaching systemic changes. It is not just the economy that is being transformed, but society itself, and five of the ten applicant countries are building new nationhood at the same time.

Economic transition has been extensively studied, albeit over a fairly brief period of history, and has resulted in a broad consensus on both the indicators of economic performance and how countries measure up. It is much harder to define and measure the quality of political life, however. Many aspects of transition may require a generation of change to consolidate patterns of interest determination among the peoples of CEE and also perceptions of the legitimacy of their political choices among outside observers such as those in the EU. Furthermore, while the EU's global judgments are based principally on analysis of the extent to which its criteria have been met, there is also a forward-looking component in judging how swiftly countries might move forward over the course of potential negotiations. Even discounting political interests of member states, complete objectivity is difficult to achieve.

Democratization

Attachment to the principles of 'liberty, democracy, respect for human rights and fundamental freedoms, and the rule of law' (Article F of the Treaty on European Union) is a defining feature of the European Union, and at Amsterdam Article O of the Treaty on European Union was modified to make respect of these principles an explicit condition for membership. For countries in transition, being accepted by the EU is important in setting a seal on their transition to democracy, just as it was for the Mediterranean countries emerging from dictatorship. However, establishing a clear set of criteria by which to measure the quality of democracy is very difficult, especially for countries that are engaged in a transformation of their political life in its widest sense.

There are general methodological problems in trying to measure the extent of democracy, the rule of law, respect for human rights and treatment of minorities in any state. In the case of the CEE countries, this task is complicated by the effects of the historical legacy of the communist period on political life and the diverse systems of governance that have emerged in post-socialist countries. For these reasons, there is less clarity and less consensus about political change than there is about economic transition in the region.

Recognition of this difficulty in assessing the extent of democratic change may, in part, underlie the Commission's judgment that only one country – Slovakia – has failed to meet the democratic criteria. In the case of Slovakia, there is a strong international consensus on the inadequacies of the functioning of democracy, whereas in other cases, where questions remain about the robustness or fragility of the democratic transition but where the trends are in the right direction, the condition is deemed to have been met.

It is also difficult to judge the effect of institutional overhang on the quality and stability of political institutions. The pre-1989 economic and political orders left a complex institutional legacy which can have a considerable impact on expectations and patterns of conduct (Hausner et al. 1995). Implementation of policy is affected when, for example, expectations of the proper scope and potential effectiveness of policies are different from those in the West. Similarly, views of the appropriate role of the state are different in societies that are still undergoing a contest about governance and regulation following more than a generation of central planning (Schöpflin 1996). Moreover, these countries are engaged in simultaneous economic and political transitions. It is problematic to try to assess the stability of political institutions in countries that are in the process of reforming those same institutions and finding their own balance between the sometimes conflicting demands of introducing markets and democracy simultaneously (Crawford 1995).

All ten of the applicants for EU membership have passed the point of no return to communism, but they exhibit considerable diversity in how cleanly they have broken with past patterns of governance and in how closely they resemble the different models of democracy existing across the EU. They all have formal procedures in place for the main features of democratic government, from free and fair elections to separation of powers, although not all of the procedures have been fully implemented (Kaldor and Vejvoda 1997). Nevertheless, the fact that democratic institutions are in place in all the CEE countries is itself a major achievement, and indicates the extent to which the CEE-10 have shed the legacy of authoritarianism.

However, these formal procedures are not all that is required to conform with European norms; rather, any assessment rests on a broad judgment about the basic quality of political life (Batt 1996). Making a broad judgment of this kind requires attention not only to the formal, procedural elements of democracy, but also to how they are put into practice and other more substantive features of a consolidated democracy. These elements of 'substantive democracy' range from independence of the media and the way human rights are perceived to the existence of an active civil society (see Kaldor and Vejvoda 1997). Linz and Stepan (1996) define five 'arenas of democracy': a lively civil society, a relatively autonomous political society, a rule of law, a usable state and an economic society. The EU has to consider how these features should be ranked in importance, and whether they can provide a picture of relative progress among the CEE-10.

In its *avis*, the European Commission has given its own judgment of how each of the applicants has progressed in general terms, but no analytical framework is provided to justify the assertions made. The *avis* describe political institutions of each country, and state that the aim is to assess how democracy works in practice by using a series of detailed criteria on the exercise of various rights and freedoms. However, the criteria used are not always made explicit, and the comments within each opinion are often vague. The Commission is known to have drawn on a range of sources, such as reports of its delegations, those of member states and reports by NGOs, but none of these is referred to in the *avis* or summaries.

The Commission reports on the three main conditions laid out at Copenhagen, and concludes that only Slovakia fails to satisfy them, although it calls for improvements in the practice of democracy and protection of minorities in a number of countries. In looking at democracy and the rule of law, the Commission judges that all of the applicant countries have flaws in the rule of law, and three (Romania, Bulgaria and Slovakia) lack the stability of institutions required for the proper functioning of public authorities and consolidating democracy. However, the progress achieved by Bulgaria and Romania since their changes of government in 1997 is noted, whereas the Commission explicitly points to a number of continued failings in this area in Slovakia.

In summarizing its views on Slovakia, the Commission states that it is 'concerned that the rule of law and democracy are not yet sufficiently deeply rooted ... A democracy cannot be considered stable if the respective rights and obligations of institutions such as the presidency, the constitutional court or the central referendum commission can be put into question by the government itself and if the legitimate role of the opposition in parliamentary committees is not accepted.' Despite the Commission's concerns about stability of institutions in Romania and Bulgaria, they are judged to meet the democracy criteria. This seems to be the right judgment, but it may also reflect the Commission's concern not to apply too strongly a condition where decisions on the precise cut-off mark in time are difficult, particularly given the changes following the last elections in both countries.

On human rights there are a few specific concerns about individual countries, such as the treatment of children in state institutions in Romania and the independence of radio and television in some of the countries. Respect for minorities is seen as problematic in a number of applicant states; in particular, Slovakia is criticized on problems in the exercise of rights by the Hungarian minority, and the rate of naturalization of non-citizens in Estonia and Latvia (principally the Russian-speaking minorities) is seen as too slow. Nevertheless, integration of minorities into society is regarded as satisfactory in general, although reference is made to discrimination against the Roma across the region. The fact that Estonia was recommended to start negotiations and Latvia was not is important in showing that for the Commission the issue of the Russian minorities is not determinant for these countries' chances of joining.

Transition to a market economy
The ten CEE applicant countries all adopted the goal of transition to a market economy, but they have not followed identical policy routes and have had widely varying degrees of success. While there are many on-going debates about the best policy routes for transition and the most appropriate indicators of transition, there is fairly widespread consensus on the relative success of different countries. Recent reports by international institutions including the EBRD and World Bank point to a similar ranking of the CEE economies, although they do not draw conclusions about readiness for EU membership.

In most analyses of transition, the Visegrad-4 and Slovenia tend to stand out as more advanced in economic transition than the other applicant countries. The Czech Republic, Hungary and Slovenia are the only countries among the CEE-10 designated by the World Bank as 'upper middle income' economies, the rest being 'lower middle income'. Along with Poland and Slovakia, these countries are also placed in the most advanced group of economies in transition on the World Bank's classification.

The Baltic states began transition later, and economic assessments tend to put them in a category below the Visegrad countries, but views on their economies are changing as they close the gap with the initial leaders in reform. Despite the massive drops in output and high inflation following their independence in 1991, they made relatively rapid progress, and the economic distinctions between the Baltic states and the central European countries are growing finer. Estonia is generally regarded as having made the fastest and most steady progress, both in stabilization and in restructuring its economy, but the distinctions between its performance and that of Latvia and Lithuania are now not great.

Ranked below the Baltics are Romania and Bulgaria, although the gap between these two economies has widened considerably since 1996. The inconsistency of economic reforms and patchiness in their implementation under the Iliescu administration prior to 1996 have caused Romania to lag behind, despite the determined efforts made by its new reforming government. The severity of the 1996–7 economic crisis in Bulgaria has forced the new government to implement radical reforms, but it now lags in transition rankings.

The economic conditions for accession
In addition to the condition of ability to take on the *acquis communautaire*, the Commission was required to assess whether the applicants have functioning market economies and whether they have the capacity to cope with competitive pressure and market forces within the Union. The Commission judges that none of the applicants fully meets these two conditions. Given this overall view, it then assesses which countries are close enough to being market economies and which will be able to cope with competitive pressures in the medium run. Making this assessment involves an element of guesswork, and there is inevitably scope for argument about the point at which the Commission has drawn a dividing line between those who should enter negotiations and those who are not ready.

In judging whether the applicants have functioning market economies, the Commission draws on many of the standard, accepted indicators of macroeconomic performance and stability of transition. Some of the criteria it states it will use in its analysis are open to question; in the Commission's view, for example, there should be an absence of significant barriers to entry and exit and a broad consensus on economic policy. This is a little strange: are Western economies that have many sectors with significant entry barriers no longer to be classified as market economies? Similarly, are major economic policy debates not perhaps a good indicator of an open society? The EU is, after all, itself the locus of fierce economic debates about the single currency.

These criticisms apart, the Commission's assessment of the transition to a market economy represents a fairly standard analysis of transition. Although it does not give the sources for its analysis, the Commission will have drawn on many of the key studies in this area, including the work of the main international institutions. There is a reasonably detailed assessment for each country although these vary between analysis, description and assertion, and some areas (notably enterprise restructuring) receive rather brief coverage. It would be easier to assess the validity of particular assertions if more detail or references were given, but, as the Commission does not differ strongly from other main transition analyses, its *avis* are unlikely to be subject to detailed criticism on this basis. In this sense, the EU has an easier job in judging the economies of the applicants than it does in judging their political development because of much wider agreement on what are the key issues in transition and how countries have performed on them.

The Commission concludes that the five front-runners – the Czech Republic, Estonia, Hungary, Poland and Slovenia – are essentially already functioning market economies, although features such as capital markets need further development and maturity. Slovakia is judged to come very close to being a market economy; the other four economies are expected to achieve this condition early in the next century. This judgment may suggest that the Commission does not expect the lagging four (Bulgaria, Latvia, Lithuania and Romania) to come close enough to meeting this condition for negotiations to start quickly.

Applying the second condition (the capacity to cope with competitive pressure and market forces within the EU) is less straightforward, not only because it is forward-looking but also because a serious assessment would require an in-depth analysis of each country's competitiveness, and of the ability of each country's enterprises to take on the Single Market *acquis* and remain competitive. The Commission recognizes that there are difficulties in assessing this condition, but it introduces some questionable criteria in making its assessment, including the proportion of small firms in each economy and whether each has a 'sufficient' quantity of human and physical capital. Given that the proportion of small and medium-sized enterprises (SMEs) varies considerably across market economies, the justification for this criterion is unclear, and the latter condition is not defining in terms of ability to compete.

48

However, the main weakness in analysing ability to compete is that the Commission provides no in-depth assessment of enterprises' ability to take on Single Market requirements and its likely impact on their competitiveness. Such an assessment would require a large study, but the general lack of work in this area creates a critical gap in understanding of the impact of enlargement on the accession countries and hence of the appropriate policy approach, especially for those countries that are many years away from joining the EU.

Trade integration is an important indicator of ability to compete, and the Commission recognizes that there has been substantial integration, while expressing concern at the functioning of capital markets, the application of competition rules and the state of infrastructure, and of progress in privatization in some countries. It also comments that wage levels remain low, presumably as a positive indicator of ability to compete. Given the difficulties with this condition, the Commission states that implementation of the Single Market White Paper measures represents both 'an approximate yardstick for the applicants' degree of preparedness' and an essential method of preparation for membership. This view suggests that it is difficult to distinguish this second condition from the third, general enlargement, condition of ability to take on the *acquis communautaire*.

The Commission's statement that applicants should have implemented all 1,400 elements of the Single Market White Paper prior to accession appears to be pre-empting negotiating decisions (see Chapter 5). Moreover, while it is fairly straightforward to assess legislative and institutional implementation of the Single Market measures, assessing adoption and impact at enterprise level is very difficult. Furthermore, if enterprises were judged to be unable to compete if they took on the Single Market *acquis*, it may not be appropriate to attempt to implement this *acquis* in the lagging transition economies in the short to medium run.

In its conclusions, the Commission expects Hungary and Poland to satisfy this second economic condition in the medium term on their current course, while the Czech Republic, Slovenia and Slovakia should be able to do so if they strengthen their efforts. Estonia is judged to be close to the latter group, but the Commission points to problems with its large external imbalance and judges that it would not yet be able to withstand competitive pressures. Given its trade deficit, the UK could well have been excluded on this condition in 1973. Latvia, Lithuania and Romania are judged to require further consolidation, while Bulgaria is expected to join them in the next decade on its present course.

Overall, on the two economic conditions, the Commission splits the six most advanced applicants into three groups: Hungary and Poland come closest, with the Czech Republic and Slovenia not far behind, while Estonia does not quite meet the competitive pressure criterion and Slovakia does not quite meet the market economy criterion.

Assuming the obligations of membership

Being able to take on the *acquis communautaire* and adhere to the aims of political, economic and monetary union is the most complex requirement, and it has received the most attention from the Commission. The most detail on the individual countries is presented in this areas in the *avis*, with conclusions on sectors ranging from the four freedoms of the Single Market to the second stage of EMU to external policy. The emphasis on this area results from its being the key focus of the pre-accession strategy (see Chapter 3), but it is also much easier to measure progress in taking on the *acquis* than to evaluate difficult issues such as long-term competitiveness and quality of democracy.

Applicants are expected to be ready, willing and able to take on the whole *acquis* on accession. The Commission judges countries' capacity to take on the obligations of membership by assessing in some detail applicants' progress in implementing the Europe Agreements, the Single Market White Paper and other parts of the *acquis*. The Commission's assessment is that individual countries' progress has been uneven across the different areas of integration activity. Only Hungary is regarded as having made satisfactory progress in all three areas of implementation. Poland, Slovakia, the Czech Republic and Slovenia have run into problems with the Europe Agreement; in particular, Poland and the Czech Republic have had a number of trade disputes with the EU in the Association Council, and Slovenia was slow to ratify its Europe Agreement. Only Hungary, Poland and the Czech Republic are judged to have made satisfactory progress in implementing the Single Market legislation, and all except Hungary and the Czech Republic are urged to step up their efforts in taking on other parts of the *acquis*. The Commission also points to a lack of structures to apply new regulations (from environmental inspections to banking supervision) throughout the region, and to widespread corruption.

The relative lack of progress on the rest of the *acquis* is unsurprising given that transposition of Single Market legislation has so far been the main focus of CEE efforts. However, the *avis* make it clear that there have been major problems in transposing even the Single Market White

Paper directives into national law. The Commission takes the problems with administrative and judicial capacity to apply the *acquis* identified in the *avis* as the starting point for recommending that 30% of Phare resources be focused on training in this area.

Looking in more detail at adaptation to the Single Market *acquis*, the Commission draws most attention to the areas of telecommunications, the environment, transport, employment and social affairs, regional policy and cohesion, agriculture, energy, and border controls. In each area there is a description of current circumstances and an assessment of how near the country is to EU standards and policy norms. Progress in these areas is uneven across most of the countries, although Bulgaria and Romania come out worse than the others on almost all counts, so judgments in this area concur with their places in the overall ranking. Hungary generally emerges best in the Commission's comments, although like all the applicants it has major environmental problems.

All the countries are very far from EU environmental standards across a whole range of areas, including waste, water and air quality. The Commission points to the need for massive investment across the region and a strengthening of administrative capacity to enforce legislation. Even the countries that receive the most favourable comments in this area (notably Estonia and the Czech Republic) are expected to achieve full compliance with the *acquis* only in the long term. Most of the other countries will reach EU standards only in the very long term, even with substantial investment. This assessment suggests that environmental problems are not only a key area for EU public investment (as the Commission proposes for use of Phare funds), but could be an important reason for negotiating transitional measures, although this will be controversial.

The picture on energy is considerably more mixed, however, despite the overlap of issues between these two areas. Partly this is because the Commission looks primarily at compatibility with energy policy, without explicitly linking production and usage with environmental issues in the *avis*. Bulgaria and Romania have major adjustments to make in reorganizing their energy sectors to comply with EU policies in both energy itself and competition law. The Commission raises concerns about nuclear safety across the region, another area to be addressed through the Accession Partnerships.

Similarly, coverage of transport policy in the *avis* does not really consider links with environmental policy objectives. The countries suffer from similar problems in this area, and the Commission focuses on the need for investment to lay the foundations for a trans-European transport network across old and new member states for effective functioning of the Single Market. Transport safety seems to be insufficiently supervised across the region because of inadequate administrative structures.

In telecommunications, there is a wide gap between the state of both policies and infrastructure in Estonia, Hungary, Latvia, the Czech Republic and Slovenia, which are judged to be close to EU norms, and the rest, which are far from them. Most of the problems in upgrading and expanding the telecoms infrastructure seem to relate to a lack of investment owing to slow demonopolization and privatization.

Employment and social affairs (including health and safety at work) are seen as unproblematic areas in most countries except Bulgaria, Romania and Slovakia. It has been argued that this is an area where new members could join with transitional periods, applying product standards to their trade in the Single Market, but leaving process standards until later (Smith et al. 1996). However, the assessment provided in the *avis* suggests that applicants are generally not very far from EU standards on the social side at least (although environmental standards are another matter, as discussed above).

Assessments of the administrative structures in regional policy and agriculture are important because these are key areas to receive EU funds prior to and on accession. Overall, only Bulgaria and Romania seem likely to have major problems with using regional aid funds, but they and the three Baltic states and Slovenia would probably find it difficult to apply the CAP without a fundamental reform and restructuring of their agricultural sectors.

When looking at countries' ability to control policy on their borders, the Commission clearly found it very difficult to assess the current state of affairs. This is obviously a key area in applying EU policy in the first and third pillars, yet the Commission commits itself to an assessment on only four of the countries (the Czech Republic, Hungary, Poland and Slovenia), all of which are judged to be able to remove border controls in the medium term. When the other countries will be able to do so is uncertain.

Looking beyond the Single Market, the Commission considers whether countries will be in a position to apply the *acquis* in the second and third pillars, and the third stage of EMU. The second pillar presents no problems for any applicant, which doubtless says more about the limited nature of the pillar than about applicants' capacities in this area. Their specific obligations under the pillar have been few and the applicants all made considerable efforts to resolve issues such as territorial disputes and control regimes as part of their bids to join NATO. Applying the third pillar, on the other hand, would be problematic for the Baltic states, Romania and Bulgaria, mainly because of institutional inadequacies and lack of experience in dealing with many of the transnational problems involved.

Ability to participate in the third stage of economic and monetary union correlates closely with countries' performances in economic transition; this is unsurprising given that joining EMU depends on sustaining the convergence criteria, coordinating economic policy and liberalizing capital movements fully. Poland, Hungary, the Czech Republic and Estonia are judged to be unlikely to face problems in joining in the medium term, although the Commission is careful to point out that meeting EMU criteria is not a condition for membership. The other countries would have problems of varying degrees of severity in accordance with their need for structural reform.

In addition to the comments on the adequacy of institutional structures in various areas of the *acquis*, the Commission covers the applicants' administrative and legal capacities in detail. On the administrative side, Hungary is rated as closest to being able to apply the *acquis*, and all the others need varying degrees of reform effort, with Romania and Bulgaria having the most work to do. On the legal side, however, there is more uncertainty in the *avis* as to capacity. The Commission states that it cannot assess judicial systems adequately in most of the countries, and leaves open the question of when most of them will be able to apply the *acquis* effectively. This area highlights perhaps most sharply the different status of the CEE countries from most previous applicants in terms of readiness to integrate with EU structures. The fundamental systemic changes of postcommunist transition make it difficult even to judge the scale of the problems that are likely to be encountered in adopting the whole *acquis* in many countries.

Conclusions

On the basis of its *avis*, the Commission recommended opening negotiations with five countries: the Czech Republic, Estonia, Hungary, Poland and Slovenia (although it is known there was a debate within the Commission about including Estonia and Slovenia). Although the Commission does not explicitly rank the ten countries in Agenda 2000, its assessment of relative readiness is clear from a comparison of the *avis*. On the overall economic and *acquis* conditions taken together, Hungary comes first, followed in joint second place by the Czech Republic and Poland. Slovenia is next, then Estonia, fairly closely followed by Slovakia, Latvia and Lithuania. Bulgaria and Romania are clearly well behind the others.

These rankings are not significantly different from the transition rankings derived from other analyses and are not very controversial. However, Latvia and Lithuania argue that they are not sufficiently far behind Estonia to justify being excluded, while Slovakia rejects criticism of its democratic functioning. With the exception of Slovakia, it is unclear whether the additional Copenhagen conditions resulted in different outcomes than judging ability to take on the *acquis communautaire* alone would have done, although they contribute to the exclusion of Latvia and Lithuania. Member states are unlikely to disagree much with the Commission's overall ranking of applicants' readiness to join; however, there is more argument about how many countries should start negotiations, as is discussed in the next chapter.

Chapter 5

The way ahead: opening negotiations and reinforcing the pre-accession strategy

Introduction

Agenda 2000 aims to offer a 'clear and coherent vision of the European Union as it enters the 21st century'. Consequently, it not only contains the ten *avis* on the applications from CEE, but also considers EU development and policy reform, future financing, and continuing pre-accession support for the applicant countries. The Intergovernmental Conference concluded at Amsterdam in June 1997 failed to confront the challenge of outlining the structure and functioning of a 26-member-state EU or of providing a strategy for getting there. Agenda 2000 confronts the immediate challenge of opening negotiations and of working with all the applicants to prepare for enlargement, but it offers an essentially incrementalist vision of institutional and policy reform, particularly for the CAP and regional funds. It envisages an enlarged EU based fully on the existing *acquis communautaire*, with adaptation of existing policies and institutional mechanisms to make this feasible.

In the face of lack of political will and leadership to consider and address the full implications of enlargement, this 'business as usual' approach to enlargement is not surprising and should be adequate to get the process under way. However, there remains no overall strategic view of the purpose, structure and functioning of an EU of 26-plus members. Neither has any attention been given to whether the traditional approach to enlargement, with its emphasis on full adoption of the *acquis communautaire*, is appropriate for countries at different stages of economic and political transition.

55

This chapter first addresses the issues involved in beginning negotiations and the potential timing and sequencing of accessions, and then analyses the Commission's proposals for reinforcing its pre-accession strategy. In subsequent chapters, we consider CEE attitudes towards EU accession (Chapter 6), and the EU's approach to policy and institutional reform (Chapter 7).

The differentiation debate

Even before the publication of the *avis*, a considerable behind-the-scenes debate was taking place among the EU member states about whether to start negotiations with all ten countries (the 'regatta approach') or to start with a smaller group on the basis of the *avis*. This debate should have been resolved at the Luxembourg summit in December 1997. Formal negotiations will begin in the first half of 1998 with Cyprus and the CEE countries selected at Luxembourg, following a grand opening conference.[1]

Member states disagree little with the Commission's overall ranking of applicants' relative readiness to join, but there has been considerable debate about where the line should be drawn between the countries that should and should not start negotiations. Prior to publication of the *avis*, the differentiation debate focused on arguments for and against the regatta approach, but it subsequently involved discussion of where to draw the dividing lines for starting negotiations, given the Commission's rankings. Countries will move through negotiations at different speeds, and German Foreign Minister Klaus Kinkel has promoted the idea of a *'Stadion-modell'* whereby applicants starting further behind in negotiations might overtake those further ahead. Nonetheless, the arguments for and against a common start have political importance both for the applicants and for the member states.

To some extent, the differing views on differentiation prior to Luxembourg can be categorized as the geo-political approach versus the objective or technocratic. Supporters of the former approach emphasize that eastward enlargement is primarily a political and strategic issue, and that the EU should make its commitment to the ten applicants clear in order to contribute to stability in the region and to give much-needed support to the ongoing process of reform. The objective condition of readiness to join can then be applied during the process of negotiations. The counter-

---

[1] The Luxembourg European Council decided to open formal negotiations with the five recommended by the Commission, although all the candidates will be included in a grand opening conference on 30 March.

argument is that this enlargement should follow the same basic rules as earlier enlargements, and negotiations should start only with countries that have reasonable prospects of acceding to the EU in the medium run.

However, the positions adopted by individual member states (although not always publicly) partly reflected differing geo-political priorities. Hence support from Denmark and Sweden for the regatta approach was dependent on their immediate interests in the Baltic states (and perhaps on a desire to be established as political leaders in the Baltic region). Greek support for the regatta approach reflected concern that Bulgaria and Romania should not be indefinitely excluded. By contrast, Italy's emphasis on the political primacy of enlargement may be as tied to its aims to be included in the single currency as to its interests in CEE. Indeed, since opening negotiations with all ten applicants could slow the process, it should not be assumed that the supporters of the regatta approach are actually most in favour of enlargement.

Germany's support for differentiation on the basis of the *avis* partly rests on its geo-political priorities, which are first Poland and then the Czech Republic and Hungary. However, there are tensions in German policy and different views in the German ministries about how fast Poland should join, given the potential impact of enlargement on the Community budget and on European integration. Nevertheless, Germany is likely to remain one of the strongest supporters of enlargement because its geo-political and economic interests in the rest of the CEE region are likely to remain greater than those of the other member states.

The United Kingdom and France have also supported differentiation. Britain in many ways has fewest problems with the idea of enlarging by ten countries, in that a weakening of the EU's integration dynamic is not a political issue; however, the UK is concerned about maintaining the integrity of the Single Market and achieving budgetary stringency, including substantial reform of the Common Agricultural Policy (CAP). France has been seen as ambivalent towards enlargement, and initially supported a regatta approach but then moved to support differentiation. Its initial regatta approach reflected a combination of wishing to be seen to be presenting a strategic political vision with a more pragmatic reluctance to see a swift enlargement. However, its shift in position appears to reflect a belief that a common start was unrealistic and unmanageable. Finland also abandoned its support for the regatta approach once the Commission recommended that negotiations be opened with Estonia.

The Commission's recommendations in July 1997 affected this debate by demonstrating a large gap between Bulgaria and Romania and the other eight applicants. This meant that Sweden and Denmark had a much stronger case by shifting their argument on to objective grounds, to argue that the dividing line should not have been drawn between Estonia and the other two Baltic countries but after all three. However, given the size of the group now favouring differentiation from the start, the Luxembourg decision will probably favour the Commission's five front-runners for formal negotiations.[2]

Rejection of the regatta approach should not be interpreted as a complete disregard for geo-political issues. Starting negotiations with the five countries recommended by the Commission would mean that important boundaries were being breached; the inclusion of one of the Baltic states is significant, particularly given the inevitable NATO exclusion, while the inclusion of Slovenia begins to open up the southern and Balkan direction of enlargement. Reports that Jacques Santer had supported opening negotiations with only three (the Czech Republic, Hungary and Poland) suggested a worrying dismissal of the geo-political issues, but this view did not win the day in the Commission's final decision.

Understandably, the Commission's recommendations have not been welcomed by the five applicants that were not recommended for inclusion in initial negotiations. There have been fears that 'double exclusion', with some countries rejected for early membership of both the EU and NATO within a year, will undermine transition. However, reaction to NATO's choice of only three countries has not so far been dramatic, and the impact of the EU's decision varies across the countries according to domestic political dynamics and the countries' medium-run prospects for starting negotiations and accession; governments' reactions also depend on their views on the Commission's plans for reinforcing the pre-accession strategy (see below).

Latvia and Lithuania are both in a position to use Estonia as a benchmark and could convince the EU quite soon that they had caught up with Estonia's position in May 1997. In contrast, Romania and Bulgaria are lagging well behind, with Bulgaria's position the more fragile, which may make it more difficult for that country to continue using the prospect of EU accession as a strong motivation for domestic reforms. Nonetheless, Bulgaria and Romania will have fairly clear milestones in their progress towards negotiations through annual reviews by the Commission.

---

[2] In the event, all the member states accepted differentiation from the start, but they agreed additional measures to reassure those not starting negotiations: the lagging countries will benefit from a 'catch-up' fund, and they will be involved in an 'analytical examination' of the *acquis* and their readiness to take it on.

The position of Slovakia is more difficult because rejection on political grounds is not particularly likely to shift Slovakia's political system in the direction of reform; the priority for the EU must be maintaining a political dialogue with Slovakia and promoting economic links.

The substance of negotiations

Although new members are officially required to take on the whole of the *acquis communautaire* on accession, negotiations in previous enlargements have led to complex sets of transitional periods on both sides. For example, some trade policy provisions took over a decade to be implemented for the Mediterranean countries (see Grabbe and Hughes 1998), while the EFTA accessions involved special arrangements for sensitive areas such as transport and the environment (see Avery 1994).

However, in no previous enlargement have the applicants been so far from EU norms, and the EU has itself become much more complex as the Single Market has developed and the second and third pillars have been added to it. Negotiations will thus be critical in determining how quickly CEE countries have to adapt to EU norms and how soon they receive all the attributes of membership. In Agenda 2000, the Commission appears at certain points to be pre-empting negotiations, both in its linking of aid and assistance to the negotiations through the reinforced pre-accession strategy and in its statement that applicants are expected to 'apply all elements of the White Paper (a selection of 1,400 pieces of key internal market legislation) in advance of accession'.[3]

Despite the Commission's assertions that there should be no derogations and that transitional periods must be limited in scope and duration, both sides have an incentive to negotiate transitional arrangements in a number of sensitive areas. However, there are pressures to limit their scope because of concerns on the CEE side that transitional periods should not result in less than full membership and on the EU side that they should not distort the Single Market. The most difficult and controversial issues are expected to be the Single Market *acquis*, free movement of people, agriculture, state aids, the environment and the structural funds. There are a number of potential trade-offs between these areas and with other areas, and the experience of the Europe Agreements could encourage a tough stance on the part of some of the applicants, which would lengthen the negotiating period.

[3] European Commission press release on Agenda 2000, issued 16 July 1997.

Agriculture is a key issue principally for Poland owing to its agricultural sector's size and importance in domestic politics. The EU is likely to want applicants to join the CAP only in stages and over a fairly lengthy period (see Chapter 7), while Poland's farmers will be pressing for transfers early on. Agriculture is also an issue for other CEE countries, but to a lesser extent. It is likely to be particularly important for Romania, although this has not yet featured strongly in domestic political debates owing to the remoteness of negotiations.

The wider question of financial transfers from the EU seems not to be a major issue in CEE politics yet, but negotiators will be keen to ensure equality of treatment with other applicants and with current EU members sooner rather than later. The experience of previous enlargements points to countries renegotiating financial transfers after accession. In this context, some common interests between existing and prospective members are clear: Poland and Spain, for example, have opposing interests during negotiations on the budget, but after Poland's accession they will have similar positions as medium-sized member states and net recipients.

Free movement of people will be sensitive for both sides. There is already concern in some EU member states (notably Germany and Austria, but also others on the eastern border of the EU) about the potential for migration from the East because of wage differentials and unemployment. These concerns reflect the sensitivity of these issues in domestic politics rather than being a response to perceived dangers of massive migratory flows. There has been discussion of imposing very long transitional periods before the free movement of people (particularly workers) is extended to new CEE members, although such a measure would be likely to be opposed by other member states (such as the UK) because it interferes with the Single Market.

The uncertainty surrounding the future of cooperation in justice and home affairs complicates extension of this part of the *acquis* to CEE. The Schengen Accord is to be incorporated into the first pillar for 12 of the member states once the Amsterdam Treaty is ratified, leaving only a rump third pillar covering police and judicial cooperation. The shambolic functioning of the third pillar is thus receiving attention, but it may take some time for the EU to determine its future shape and scope, which complicates the task of trying to extend it to the CEE countries. In particular, the content of the Schengen *acquis* has received little attention, and it is uncertain how difficult it will be to apply its provisions to CEE countries; these new members, unlike the UK, Ireland and Denmark, will be unable to gain an opt-out from Schengen, although long transitional periods are likely to be negotiated in some areas.

On the CEE side, a number of politically sensitive issues arise, although most seem unlikely to be changed significantly by negotiations. There is the question about free movement of people once some countries join the EU and others are left outside. This is particularly important for Hungary, but other countries also have mixed populations in border areas which are used to travelling freely across the border. Long transitions on freedom of movement for the new members would be very sensitive domestically and would be seen as denoting second-class membership. The issue of visa-free travel to the EU is extremely important to Bulgaria and Romania, and at present there seems to be little prospect of their joining the EU's common visa list for several years, perhaps not until negotiations begin. The question of allowing foreigners to buy land will be difficult for several countries, especially Slovenia and Poland, causing problems of substance as well as symbolism in negotiations. However, there is probably little room for negotiation on this issue because of the importance to the Single Market of maintaining freedom of establishment.

State aids are a concern of CEE negotiators while their governments are still reducing subsidies to heavy industry and mining. However, EU competition rules have to be applied in advance of accession under the Europe Agreements and discussions on state aids are unlikely to form a part of the intergovernmental bargaining process. Competition policy is an area of Commission competence and so is not formally part of the negotiating procedure; thus, new member states would effectively negotiate state aids bilaterally with the Commission, as happened previously.

Nevertheless, there seem to be hopes on the CEE countries' side of their being able to negotiate implicit trade-offs between restrictions on state aids and receiving EU transfers from the structural funds prior to accession; moreover, the applicants are aware of the numerous exceptions made for EU members in allowing state aids, and the Commission's proposals for the reinforced pre-accession strategy emphasize supporting investment for restructuring. The European Commission seems unlikely to agree to a formal transitional period covering all state aids, but it might be possible to negotiate sectoral arrangements for CEE industries. Under Article 92.3.A of the Treaty on European Union, current rules allow use of state aids under sectoral agreements if there are exceptional circumstances. Some CEE countries are seeking to obtain a second five-year exemption from state aid controls under this provision, which would potentially extend until after their accessions.

The applicants may also seek derogations on EU environmental and social standards until they reach a certain level of economic development. This possibility has caused concerns within member states about the potential distortion of the Single Market through the 'dumping' of products made under worse social and environmental conditions than those prevailing in the EU. As Agenda 2000 makes clear, all the applicants face major difficulties in meeting EU environmental standards even in the medium run. Resolution of competing interests and concerns here could thus be very difficult.

Timing of negotiations and accessions

As the above discussion shows, it is difficult to estimate exactly how long the first set of negotiations might take. Not only is there a series of complex and contentious issues to be agreed, but the necessary reforms on the EU side mean that different member states might have an interest at various points in slowing or blocking negotiations because of intra-EU bargaining. It cannot be assumed that all the CEE publics will support accession in the end, especially if membership is significantly delayed and there are controversial transition arrangements, although current trends suggest that no country is likely to reject membership in a referendum (see Chapter 6).

Overall, negotiations for the first five applicants and Cyprus could take between three and seven years, assuming there is no serious breakdown. Allowing at least a year for ratification, possible accession dates lie between 2002 and 2006. It is likely that not all the first five will join at the same time. Concerns are frequently expressed about Poland in particular, because of its size and the state of Polish industry and agriculture. While some of the applicants view the prospect of accession in 2005–6 as pessimistic and very unwelcome, others are more sanguine, recognizing that their economies need time to adjust. However, if slow negotiations reflected obstructive behaviour on the part of some EU members, negative political reactions could be expected in CEE.

It is more difficult to predict likely accession dates for the remaining five applicants. On current trends, Latvia and Lithuania could expect to be one to three years behind the first group. Bulgaria and Romania are currently well behind the other applicants on the economic front; given the speed of reforms undertaken by other countries, they have the potential to close the gap relatively quickly, but equally, they could continue to lag. Given the political basis for Slovakia's exclusion from negotiations, its likely negotiating or accession dates are also difficult to predict. The accession of a government more committed to democratic practices could lead to relatively rapid fulfilment of the conditions for starting negotiations, although Slovakia would have to speed up its preparations considerably if it were to join at the same time as the front-runner applicants.

Overall, Latvia and Lithuania might join in the middle or second half of the next decade, as could Slovakia, while Bulgaria and Romania are likely to join, at the earliest, in the second half of the decade and, on current trends, possibly not until the following one. During this period the EU might receive other applications for membership, in particular from other states of the former Yugoslavia, and a new applicant might even leapfrog some of the lagging members in the current set of applicants. The EU will also have to make some response to the pressure to reconsider Turkey's application.

This sketch of likely timing scenarios makes it clear that the EU is embarking on a process of enlargement that will span two decades, at the end of which it could have 30 or more members. This will be a very difficult process to manage both in terms of handling EU politics and overall development, and also in terms of the EU's relations with the different applicants. It is unlikely that the EU will draw up a strategy for the next two decades; rather, it will manage these enlargement processes sequentially. Doing so successfully is a major challenge, because an EU that encompassed 30 members would inevitably be a very different organization from the current Union.

If the momentum of the enlargement process is to be maintained, the EU should aim for swift accession for the front-runners. However, current indications are that member states are content to see the process last until 2004–5, rather than wanting to ensure that the first accessions happen around 2002. No precise date can be given in advance of negotiations, but a target date of 2002–3 would help to dynamize the process, providing a much-needed stimulus to progress on both negotiations and the EU's own reforms.

Relations with the applicants

Reinforcing the pre-accession strategy
In Agenda 2000, the Commission proposes the establishment of 'Accession Partnership' agreements with each applicant. These agreements will provide the basis for a reinforced pre-accession strategy, responding to a

general view among policy-makers that the strategy needs strengthening. The Commission is essentially proposing a common structure for all applicants, irrespective of whether they are in negotiations. This approach is in some ways attractive as it would help to avoid giving those not in negotiations a sense of being excluded from the process. Moreover, a pre-accession strategy is still needed, given that even the front-runners are at least four to eight years from accession, and the *avis* have highlighted how far all of the countries are from EU norms in most areas.

However, it is not obvious that the lagging countries have the same policy needs as the front-runners; rather, they are likely to need different and additional policy approaches. Furthermore, the proposed reinforced pre-accession strategy will overlap with the on-going process of negotiations in ways that might either pre-empt them or create conflict between the negotiations and the Accession Partnerships.

The Accession Partnerships are intended to provide a coherent, inclusive structure for the applicants' relations with the EU prior to accession. They are to be drawn up on the basis of the *avis* and in discussion with each applicant. They will identify areas for action that must be addressed either to reach a level where the Commission can recommend opening negotiations, or to join the EU. The Accession Partnerships will set out a series of objectives and a timetable for achieving them, with applicants setting up national programmes and timetables to adopt the *acquis*. The objectives will focus both on the *acquis* and on problem areas identified in the *avis*, and also on the wider Copenhagen conditions, with particular attention to democratic objectives, macroeconomic stabilization and nuclear safety. The Commission will draw up annual reports on each country's progress in meeting the partnership objectives; in the case of the countries not yet in negotiations, it will make recommendations as to whether each is now ready to begin them.

The Commission also proposes that all its financial assistance to the applicants (from Phare, the structural funds budget and agricultural support) be targeted on the objectives set out in the Accession Partnership agreements. In this context, the Commission introduces the idea of applying strict conditionality to its financial support; financial aid will depend on each country's success in meeting the objectives set out in its partnership agreement, as evaluated annually by the Commission.

It is also proposed that Phare be refocused. The severity of human resource deficiencies for implementing the *acquis* in the applicant countries, particularly the insufficiency of administrative expertise in EU matters, leads the Commission to propose that 30% of Phare funds be directed towards training for specialists in this area – broadly termed 'institution-building'. Seventy per cent of Phare funds are to be directed towards investment projects aimed at bringing enterprises and sectors up to EU standards; the Commission considers this the only means of avoiding long-run transitions. From 2000, finance will also be available from the structural funds, and the Commission suggests this should be directed principally towards infrastructure projects, particularly in environmental and transport fields.

The reaction in CEE to these proposals is mixed. There is widespread awareness of the difference in scale between Phare funds and those made available to the Mediterranean countries before and after accession. The Accession Partnerships proposed by the Commission are thus welcome as additional sources of aid, although some CEE policy-makers argue that specific funds for agriculture are not a priority and that better market access for agricultural products is a greater concern. From their point of view, the new funds will be less responsive to perceived needs as they will be spent more at the direction of the EU; Phare was previously demand-driven, whereas now national authorities will have less room to set their own priorities for use of external aid, although the accession partnership will be agreed between each country and the Commission.

There are a number of potential difficulties with the approach proposed by the Commission through the Accession Partnership agreements. The concept of financial conditionality is particularly problematic. Given that EU funds will be targeted at meeting the objectives set out in each partnership agreement, it is not obvious why failure to meet objectives should mean a withdrawal of funds. Any failure should surely receive analysis and attention as to its causes, together with proposed remedies. Given the history of failures of central planning, it would be surprising if all the EU's investment projects precisely met their targets. Furthermore, if countries that are having difficulties in meeting their targets also face a withdrawal of funds, this will open up yet wider gaps between more and less successful applicants. A more sophisticated approach to conditionality is needed.

It is also questionable whether it is appropriate to target all the EU's aid and assistance on meeting the conditions for accession. This may be an appropriate strategy for the front-runners, but for countries that are still at relatively early stages of transition – and might take more than ten years to join the EU – the principal focus of assistance should be on the central needs of political and economic transition. Furthermore, the lack of detail in many parts of the *avis* means that they may not provide an adequate basis for identifying appropriate objectives for aid policies.

The Commission also proposes coordinating with other international financial institutions to ensure that their aid complements its preparations by arranging co-financing operations with the EIB, EBRD and World Bank. As yet it is very unclear how such cooperation will work, particularly given the different overall missions of these agencies in CEE. Detailed preparations for accession are not necessarily wholly compatible with EBRD and World Bank goals for the development of post-communist economies. An internal debate is already taking place at the EBRD, for example, about the degree to which it should finance EU accession rather than concentrating on removing obstacles to private investment further east (*Financial Times*, 18 July 1997). There are also more general questions about how the new policies would operate. There are clearly areas of common interest in, for example, assisting with institutional reforms which provide the key underpinnings for investments by international agencies. But the EU and the various international financial institutions have different bureaucratic cultures and entrenched ways of working, so how effectively they will be able to work together in CEE remains open to question, especially if their different overall missions lead to conflicts of interest in project implementation.

The Commission, through the Accession Partnerships, also runs the risk of overlapping with the enlargement negotiations with the front-runners. The Commission claims it is forced to link its aid provision to negotiations through the annual reports on the partnership agreements and financial conditionality to ensure coherence. However, it is unclear how the views expressed in the annual reports can or will be coordinated with the progress of negotiations. For example, should the Accession Partnerships allow for negotiations to be slowed down or suspended if a country fails to meet its targets? Similarly, might the annual reviews duplicate or contradict decisions made in negotiations? Given the overlap with negotiations, it is likely that the member states will press for more of a role in the Accession Partnership agreements and not just leave them to the Commission, particularly as running these processes in parallel would certainly be a major departure from previous enlargement procedures. The agreements could reduce flexibility in negotiations and slow them down, even though they might be useful in maintaining pressure for reform in CEE.

Although the reinforced pre-accession strategy treats all the applicants in a similar way, the EU's budget proposals mean that the front-runners will receive substantially more aid once they join the EU (see Chapter 7). Over the budget period 2000–2006, the Commission proposes overall assistance to the applicants of 74.8bn ECU, of which the five entering negotiations would get 53.8bn ECU once they join (the year 2002 is used as a working assumption) and 3.6bn ECU before they join. The five not in negotiations would get 17.4bn ECU over the whole period. While the five lagging countries would get more Phare and structural funds aid once the others join, the proposals mean that the front-runners get three-quarters of the budget and the lagging five only one-quarter. Assuming that aid is effective, this means that the lagging five will fall increasingly behind.

No other policy measures are put forward to help all the applicants, nor are there any specific proposals for the five not in negotiations.[4] Appropriate measures here could range from opening agricultural markets to setting an indicative time-frame for the whole enlargement process. Overall, a strengthened commitment from the EU is needed, especially for the countries rejected by NATO and those lagging behind economically. For Romania and Bulgaria a critical issue is visas. They are currently the only CEE applicants whose nationals still need separate visas to travel to each EU country, and being excluded from the common visa list has become a sensitive issue domestically. Freedom to travel in the EU on a common visa would be a very important symbol of equal treatment with the other applicant countries.

A European Conference
The Commission proposes abandoning the much-criticized Structured Dialogue and establishing bilateral cooperation committees to discuss the reinforced pre-accession strategy with *ad hoc* multilateral meetings when necessary. However, Agenda 2000 also proposes a formal multilateral structure, supporting the French idea of establishing a standing European Conference on enlargement. The Commission suggests that it be used for general consultations on issues arising in the second and third pillars, but little substantive detail is provided. In the field of the common foreign and security policy (CFSP), it would be used for 'dialogue' on relations with eastern neighbours, including Russia and Ukraine, while for justice and home affairs it would 'facilitate cooperation'. Overall, the Conference would meet once a year at heads of state or government level, and at ministerial level 'where necessary'. Member states have had widely

---

[4] The Luxembourg European Council agreed to Commission proposals to create a 'catch-up' fund for the lagging countries, but the size of the fund seems likely to be small.

varying views on its potential scope. The European Conference will open in London in March 1998.

The overall concept of establishing a European Conference has been gaining support from member states as a way of including the laggards in discussions while excluding them from formal negotiations. Many member states would like to include Turkey in the Conference to provide some sort of inclusive arrangement while avoiding the issue of opening negotiations with it, but others, particularly Greece, have opposed this idea, fearing that this would make it more difficult to avoid the question of Turkey's application for membership. If Greece's opposition can be overcome, however, Turkey is likely to be included. There were also suggestions that Ukraine and Russia might have observer status in the Conference if it were a device for cooperation rather than discussion of pre-accession issues. Whether or not Turkey and other countries are included is likely to affect whether the Conference becomes more of a pre-accession instrument or a forum for dealing with wider regional issues.[5]

The idea of setting up a European Conference has received quite widespread support in CEE, although there is concern that it should have more substance than the Structured Dialogue. The front-runner countries tend to see it as a useful political framework for the overall process of enlargement, particularly for those left out of negotiations. But an immediate rider is that it would have to be more than a general discussion forum and should have real decision-making capacities. Given the range and scope of issues raised by enlargement, in terms of both the requirements of membership and its wider impact on the region, this idea deserves considerably more discussion and thought, lest the Conference become no more than a waiting-room for formal negotiations.

Used properly, the European Conference could be an important forum for dealing with issues concerning both CEE and the EU, irrespective of enlargement. There is already a common interest in working together on trans-border issues such as crime, illegal immigration and police cooperation in advance of accession; this is a question not just of the applicants adapting to EU procedures, but of their taking substantive measures to tackle these problems regardless of the state of the enlargement process.

---

[5] At Luxembourg, member states agreed to establish the European Conference. Turkey was invited to participate, but the Ankara government replied in December 1997 that it would not attend unless treated like the CEE applicants and included in the enlargement process.

However, more thought needs to be given to how practical cooperation with the applicants on second- and third-pillar issues would work, particularly as the EU-15 have experienced major problems with functioning in these areas. These are highly sensitive and complex areas, and member states' interior ministries seem to lack confidence in the data protection offered by the CEE countries; if CEE infrastructure in these areas is inadequate, member state authorities will not cooperate fully. There is clearly a need for EU expertise and investment to be used here for mutual benefit.

Conclusion

This chapter has focused on the Commission's assessments of the CEE applicants as reflected in its *avis* and on its proposals for future relations with the CEE applicants. This part of Agenda 2000 represents an attempt to take a more strategic approach to relations with the applicants than the previous pre-accession strategy did. The rankings of countries that can be derived from the *avis* are not highly controversial because they agree with rankings produced by other analyses of transition, although precisely where the dividing line should be drawn for negotiations is more controversial. There are, however, a number of difficulties with the proposed structure based on the Accession Partnership agreements, and their relationship with the process of negotiations is unclear. Furthermore, while in principle the idea of including all applicants in the same policy structure is welcome, in practice the needs of those already in negotiations and those further behind are likely to differ.

Detailed preparations for taking on the *acquis communautaire* will certainly require more resources, and the idea of focusing on implementation and enforcement of EU-compatible legislation has been welcomed in the front-runner applicant countries. However, such intensive preparations for accession may be inappropriate for the countries further behind in the processes of both transition and EU approximation. There is little in the Commission's proposals to support them in meeting more immediate needs, especially if aid is to be geared primarily to taking on the *acquis*.

On current trends, the first new members might join the EU sometime between 2002 and 2006. Present political circumstances make 2002 look optimistic; if the EU wishes to confirm its commitment to enlargement and maintain the momentum of the process, however, it should adopt 2002 as a target for the first accessions.

Chapter 6

The view from CEE: political debates and public opinion

Introduction

Across central and eastern Europe, motivations to join the EU are based on what the Union represents in geographical, political, economic and security terms. CEE countries have sought to join international organizations rapidly to facilitate and consolidate their reintegration into Western multilateral structures. As the focus of successful postwar political and economic integration in western Europe, the EU is the central international and regional organization to join. The EU is also the main source of aid, trade and investment in CEE, and the increasing economic integration between the two regions is reinforcing political and other interests in membership. The much higher living standards in EU countries than in CEE since the Second World War have led to expectations that membership will bring similar benefits to post-communist economies. For the seven applicants that have not been invited to join NATO, the implicit security guarantee that membership provides is particularly important (see Chapter 1 for a fuller discussion).

Geo-political, strategic and economic interests thus combine to draw CEE states towards the magnet of European integration. There is currently a very high degree of consensus among political actors in CEE supporting the principle of accession, and public opinion is generally in favour as well. However, implications of accession have barely begun to impinge on domestic debates. Views among both political actors and the general public about the different aspects of EU membership, as opposed to the general principle of membership, are still largely unformed, with discussion focused on the historical and geo-political reasons for joining.

The implications of membership for a whole range of policy areas will doubtless be controversial, but only the bare outlines of the political debate to come are yet visible. Some of the issues that are likely to prove problematic in negotiations have been set out in Chapter 5; other issues will also emerge in domestic political debates as knowledge and awareness grow of how accession will affect various interest groups in the applicant countries.

Because discussion of EU accession is at such a general level in CEE, it is difficult to give a comprehensive assessment of the range of views; nevertheless, a number of emerging issues can be highlighted. This chapter analyses the nature and extent of political debate on joining the EU in the ten applicant countries, and also trends in public opinion.[1]

Political debates about European integration

The scope and intensity of political debate
In all of the CEE countries, EU integration is one of the least controversial issues on the political agenda. Even in countries with generally very active political debates and vocal oppositions on domestic issues, accession is one of the few generally uncontested aims in national parliaments. This stands in contrast to the more intense debate about NATO membership in Hungary, the Czech Republic, Slovakia and Bulgaria, where there is vocal opposition to the principle of joining as well as to its implications.

However, despite the high degree of consensus on the overall *goal* of EU membership, there is already some variation in the scope and intensity of debate so far on its *implications*, and this provides pointers as to how national debates might develop. It is possible to discern emerging attitudes to issues that will be involved in EU accession, although such trends should be considered against a background of very limited overall coverage of these issues in political life in comparison with other foreign and domestic policies. In no country have all the implications of EU membership been widely recognized and discussed, and the level of knowledge about the EU and its workings is still fairly low even among elites. Moreover, in all of the countries there is very little discussion of the pros and cons of different elements of the rights and obligations of

---

[1] The discussion of policy views and political debates presented here is based on a series of interviews conducted by the authors with CEE policy-makers, journalists, academics, parliamentarians and business organizations.

71

EU membership, with such debate as there is mostly focused on the general principles that are perceived to guide EU policies.

Poland seems to be experiencing the liveliest arguments between political parties and in the press about relations with the EU, although few openly contest the aim of joining. Discussion of the implications of membership is just beginning. Right-wing parties such as the ROP (Movement for the Reconstruction of Poland) in particular hedge their support with arguments for more attention to the dangers of agricultural decline, cheap imports, cultural and religious influences and the influence of Germany, arguing for Poland to take an approach based on 'Eurorealism' rather than undiluted enthusiasm. Parties on the left (such as the PSL, parts of the SLD and the pensioners' parties) are concerned about the protection of smallholders, pensioners and other groups that will be adversely affected by transition. The issue of trade relations with the EU has been controversial for several years owing to Poland's series of high-profile disputes with the EU, and the question of agricultural trade restrictions under the Europe Agreement has been quite widely covered in the press.

Yet even in Poland there is little open Euroscepticism; arguments are concerned with being tough in negotiations and joining on favourable terms, rather than with any other form of association with the EU. Moreover, public opinion remains strongly in favour of joining both the EU and NATO. The fact that the Polish debate has gone further than the others is due partly to Poland's assertive approach to accession. Awareness of Poland's geo-political importance to the EU, especially Germany, has encouraged policy-makers and politicians to assume that it will be among the first to join, despite warnings from the EU that it is perfectly feasible that other less problematic applicants might finish negotiations first (see Chapter 5). This greater confidence about being accepted has moved debate on to more detailed questions of Polish–EU relations and the terms of membership, while other countries (particularly Bulgaria and Romania) are still at the earlier stage of discussing whether and when they might be able to join.

In contrast to Poland, there is much less debate about EU issues in Hungary between the parties and in the press. The degree of consensus is very high on both the overall aim and Hungary's preparations so far for joining; European integration is one of the few policy areas where parliamentary parties usually agree. Debate could develop over negotiating strategies, however, owing to divisions in the Hungarian Socialist Party (currently in a coalition government with the Liberals). In addition,

FIDESZ leader Viktor Orban argues that Hungary has to be tough in negotiations and prove that it is in the national interest to join. The only opponents of accession are small parties outside parliament on the extreme right and left, although in parliament the leader of the populist Smallholders' Party has expressed doubts about aspects of integration.

Until the economic crisis in summer 1997, there was considerable confidence in the Czech Republic about getting into the EU and its overall progress in transition, and both NATO and EU membership remain the top foreign policy priorities for the Czech government. Open and high-profile criticism of EU developments from Vaclav Klaus when he was prime minister stimulated debate in the Czech Republic about issues such as monetary union and the social dimension of EU policies. The main opposition party, the Social Democrats, argues for a more positive attitude towards EU integration, but the opposition seems to be less involved in policy-making and less informed on European integration matters than in some other applicant countries, despite the fractiousness of the governing centre–right coalition. This affects the extent of the debate; there is a general consensus on the goal of EU integration, but little discussion of the details. The apparent marginalization of the opposition parties in deciding preparations for accession might provide more scope for disagreement as negotiations proceed because the government has not built up a domestic consensus for its negotiating positions. In addition, there is overt opposition to joining from the Communist and Republican parties in parliament, which together received some 18% of the vote in 1996.

In Slovakia the goal of EU membership is rarely openly opposed in itself, but progress in integration tends to become part of the intense contestation of politics. The last few years have seen the issue of EU and NATO accession become increasingly a part of the political rivalry between the main governing party, HZDS (Movement for a Democratic Slovakia), and the opposition parties. Each side has blamed the other for any signs of Slovak exclusion from Euro-Atlantic structures, the opposition criticizing Prime Minister Vladimir Meciar's policies and undemocratic practices and the government claiming that exclusion has occurred because the opposition has presented a negative view of Slovakia to outsiders. However, the opposition has so far failed to use exclusion from NATO and criticism of the government by the EU effectively for domestic political gain. Partly this is because of the prime minister's control of the media, but it is also symptomatic of the opposition parties' inability to unite against the government; the SLD

(Party of the Democratic Left) has been particularly unwilling to sustain alliances with the non-socialist opposition parties.

The Slovak opposition is clearly more willing to implement both political and economic reforms to prepare for EU membership than is the governing coalition, but the requirements of membership have not been much discussed (or even understood) because debate has focused so much on domestic issues and inter-party battles. Views of EU accession within HZDS are unclear, but there seems to be potential for intra-party divisions once the requirements of membership start to impinge more, given its largely rural and low-skilled constituency. HZDS is in a coalition government with the SNS (Slovak National Party) and ZRS (Association of Slovak Workers); although neither party has so far openly opposed accession in principle, their programmes will clearly conflict with aspects of membership, and both parties are against NATO membership.

EU accession is generally supported by political parties in Slovenia, but there seems to be less confidence about joining than in the other front-runners in transition. This can be explained partly by the long-running dispute with Italy over property restitution that blocked Slovenia's application until June 1996. Slow implementation of EU obligations has continued since; for example, Slovenia's Europe Agreement has still not been ratified (see Chapter 4).

There seem to be more doubts about membership among the elite than in the other countries, particularly concerning Slovenia's status and identity as a small nation (see Milanovich 1997). Slovenia's unhappy experience as part of the Yugoslav federation seems to have coloured views of its prospects within the EU; although membership is seen as a way of ensuring escape from the postwar troubles still besetting the rest of the former Yugoslavia, there are also concerns that such a small country might be overlooked in the EU framework or its identity threatened. There are additional undercurrents in the Slovene debate owing to fears of foreign interference, particularly foreigners buying property, partly because of the country's small physical size and continuing tensions in its relations with Italy.

For the three Baltic states, the security implications are a major attraction of EU membership, and this seems to have a unifying effect on views on accession. There is a general consensus on EU policy and preparations so far in all three countries, no doubt reinforced in Estonia and Latvia by the tendency of their governments to comprise grand coalitions of numerous parties. Overall, until recently there has been a surprisingly high level of consensus among political parties in the Baltics on preparations for EU accession given the popular scepticism revealed in opinion polls (see below).

Political debates on preparations for accession have become more intense in Latvia and Lithuania since publication of the Commission's *avis* and its recommendation that negotiations be started with Estonia but not with the other two countries. Disappointment at the recommendations was accompanied by criticism in the domestic press, which blamed the decisions on a Commission failure to take into account economic progress in the last year. Some criticism also rebounded on the governments, and the Latvian minister for EU affairs was replaced. Nevertheless, even if prospects for accession are now receiving more attention, debate on individual aspects of membership is still at a very early stage.

There is also scope for more debate among the Estonian elite. There has already been criticism in Tallinn of the contrast between the relatively radical approach taken by Estonia to marketization and liberalization in transition and what are seen as EU attempts to protect and subsidize parts of its economy. Concern has been expressed about the prospect of Estonia having to re-erect trade barriers against third countries when it joins the Single Market, and the CAP has been criticized for subsidizing EU farmers unfairly in comparison with their Estonian counterparts, for example. As yet, these criticisms of the EU have not threatened the political consensus on accession, but negotiations are likely to bring out the tensions rather more acutely.

There is strong elite support in Romania for joining both the EU and NATO, but there was very little discussion of EU issues while prospects for joining NATO dominated discussion of Euro-Atlantic integration. Following the Alliance's decision at Madrid in June 1997 not to invite Romania to join in 1999, debate has continued to focus on the rejection for NATO's first round, although publication of the Commission's opinion on Romania's application has called more attention to EU accession. A few fringe parties oppose EU membership, but overall there is a strong sense of inevitability about joining the EU, a belief that historically Romania belongs to Europe, and public support is extremely high. However, there is hardly any debate about the implications of EU membership. This may reflect the fact that the EU seems rather remote, and there are more immediate pressures while Romania is undergoing major reforms under the new government.

In Bulgaria, the issue of EU membership has a higher profile than the NATO issue, and there are hardly any dissenting voices on accession. Discussion still centres on whether or not Bulgaria will be able to join, with very little media attention to concrete developments in relations with the EU (Shikova and Nikolov 1997); moreover, there seems to have been a lack of realistic debate about the possibility of Bulgaria's exclusion from initial negotiations right up to the publication of Agenda 2000. At present, Bulgaria seems to have the highest degree of consensus on EU accession among political actors; the issues surrounding member-ship are not a major part of political debate, even though much work is being done behind the scenes to prepare for meeting the EU's conditions.

In both Romania and Bulgaria, a widely discussed issue concerning the EU is the absence of Bulgaria and Romania (but not the other applicant countries) from the EU's common visa list. Restrictions on freedom to travel within the EU are thus already an important issue, and there are perceptions of discrimination by the EU against Bulgarian and Romanian citizens.

Outside party debates in all the CEE countries, other political actors are also generally in favour of accession. At the moment large businesses seem to be generally supportive of integration efforts, but uncompetitive industries may be less keen later on in the process when negotiations make clearer the implications of joining the Single Market. In sensitive sectors (especially agriculture) there is some bitterness about the restrictions imposed on exports by the Europe Agreements, and EU competition policy has already encouraged the removal of state aids, whether open or hidden, to declining sectors. Environmental standards and health and safety issues are also likely to provoke opposition from businesses, and the potential for negotiating transitional periods in these areas could attract significant lobbying efforts.

Future development of political debates
With a few exceptions, then, it is only fringe parties outside parliament who argue openly against the principle of joining the EU. However, this lack of opposition to the goal of accession is in the context of very limited debate about what joining the EU will actually entail. Debate about the implications of accession is likely to grow once negotiations begin and awareness of the EU's activities becomes more widespread. It has already been stimulated by the publication of the European Com-mission's *avis*, which encouraged greater press coverage and increased awareness of the move towards negotiations. The process of negotiations will provide further scope for debate. Once formal talks are under way, the political debate in those countries involved will be affected both by the substance of negotiations and by the geo-political impact on the

region of how the EU handles the enlargement process. In those countries still waiting to join negotiations, the focus is likely to be progress in meeting EU requirements as detailed in the Accession Partnerships, as well as the annual reviews by the Commission which could result in a recommendation to start negotiations. Other fora surrounding negotiations, such as the European Conference, could also stimulate more discussion of the issues raised by integration.

As well as influencing foreign policy, the EU will progressively affect a whole range of domestic policy issues even before membership, as countries approximate regulations, standards and overall policies to fit EU norms (see Chapter 5); so discussion can be expected to grow and become more informed. Criticism of some aspects of the EU can be expected to increase, although there will also be more voices pointing out the benefits of membership as the discussion becomes more informed. Views on EU accession can be expected to become more sharply defined once it becomes clearer which policy areas will be affected and who might lose out from integration. Some of the populist parties at the far right and left of the political spectrum could well become more openly opposed to specific aspects of European integration, if not actually to eventual accession itself, as the demands of membership become more pressing later on in the process.

Debate could start to focus on general issues such as national interests and sovereignty, the costs and benefits of membership, and the potential for developing eastward as well as westward links. There could also be more debate as the detailed requirements of Single Market legislation become more apparent. At present the impact of the EU on domestic policy reforms does not seem to be a significant political issue, and preparations for joining the EU seem not to be distinguished much from efforts to rejoin all Western structures. For example, the changes effected by implementation of the Single Market White Paper have not so far been very controversial within countries; this is because they have not had obvious and widespread effects, and most have not been specifically attached to EU membership, as opposed to being part of overall transition.

However, there could be a cumulative effect as the extent to which the EU will affect a whole range of policies becomes more apparent. Controversy over the effects of the Europe Agreements on agricultural trade shows the potential for adverse reaction to EU measures. The cause of those whose lot has been made worse rather than better by transition (most notably those working in agriculture, pensioners and the unemployed) could be articulated in opposition to joining if a more

77

explicit connection is drawn between economic reforms and EU membership. In addition, as the actual impact of EU accession becomes more visible, opposition from those disadvantaged by it is likely to emerge in some form in the political debate, although this may differ in extent and form in the individual countries, and (as is discussed in Chapter 5) nobody is yet sure what effects taking on the full *acquis* will have on CEE economies.

In addition to the adoption of Single Market legislation, there are other potentially controversial issues that are not much discussed yet. The question of whether foreigners should be able to buy property freely is particularly sensitive in Poland, the Czech Republic and Slovenia, for example. The sequencing of accessions could bring out several problems. In Hungary the implications of joining the Schengen area could be very controversial, as Budapest would have to restrict the currently visa-free access of Hungarian minorities living in the neighbouring states of Slovakia, Romania and Ukraine if it joined first. In all the countries borders could be problematic issues, as they will have to be policed more effectively and more controls will have to be put on the movement of people and goods when they become the eastern frontier of the EU.

These sorts of issues touch the daily lives of the population more than the overall thrust of foreign policy has done, and could awaken anti-EU sentiment if mishandled; as the extent to which previously wholly domestic questions are decided at EU level becomes clearer, it could fuel nationalistic arguments about sovereignty, for example. However, on the positive side, the potential benefits of membership will also be more thoroughly aired, particularly financial transfers from the EU and increased trade and investment. Overall, national preferences in different policy areas are likely to become more clearly defined, just as has happened in existing member states. More variety in the scope and intensity of CEE debates about accession can thus be expected to emerge as negotiations proceed, given the range of different national sensitivities.

What kind of member states will this make the CEE countries? Some trends in the political debate point to emerging attitudes towards development of the EU. Understandably, most of the countries are concerned to protect the position of small members within the Union. Similarly, there is some wariness about moves towards political union in those countries with experience of federations or the Soviet Union (the Czech Republic, Slovakia, Slovenia and the Baltic states). Doubts about the potential scope of integration seem most widespread in these countries, whereas Poland and Hungary seem more pro-integrationist.

There are some indications about preferences on specific EU policy approaches. In Estonia and the Czech Republic, the countries that have taken the most avowedly free-market approaches to transition, concerns have been expressed about protectionist tendencies and the social-democratic elements of the EU and its policies. There has also been some debate on this issue in Poland between those who see the EU as overly beholden to social democracy and those who see it as too free-market. There is opposition to EMU in some of the right-wing parties in Poland and the Czech Republic, but little debate in other countries. There seems to be fairly widespread recognition that joining the single currency is inevitable, not just because of accession, but because of trade links with the prospective EU zone; however, national currencies are important symbols of hard-won independence in the region. On the budget, Poland would be likely to form alliances with net recipients such as Spain to demand more transfers, especially through the structural funds. Regional policy issues could also be important in countries such as Estonia and Hungary owing to their different concerns about minorities.

Expectations of timing and sequencing
Expectations of how long negotiations might take and when countries might join seem to be a function of closeness to preparations and level of knowledge; those involved in detailed preparations are generally much more cautious and prone to expect a long period for negotiating than those whose knowledge is confined to the overall direction of foreign policy. However, in all of the countries there would be considerable disappointment if the first accessions do not occur before 2005; it is very important that the enlargement process is seen to move ahead, even if some countries join considerably later than others. Frustration is likely to set in if the process is attenuated and the time-frame left unclear.

In the five front-runner countries (the Czech Republic, Estonia, Hungary, Poland and Slovenia) political actors generally expect to join sometime between 2002 and 2005. However, the promises of Chirac and Kohl of accession in 2000 have been more widely accepted as credible in Poland, where disappointment will be greater at the slow speed of the process, while views in the Czech Republic are more sanguine on slower accession. Entry of the first new members after 2005 would also be disappointing to Latvia and Lithuania because it would set back their chances too.

In Slovakia, both civil servants and opposition politicians expect the country to join the first wave of applicants very quickly if there is a change of government, and they are still hoping for accession around

2003. Given the slow pace of preparations and the major gaps in administrative resources high-lighted by Slovakia's *avis*, these expectations could prove to be unrealistic. Although the main bar to opening negotiations with Slovakia is its deficiencies in democratic institutions, the gap with the five front-runner countries' preparations is likely to widen further once negotiations begin. Romanians seem to expect a considerably later date for accession, perhaps 2007 (although this still looks unrealistic, as is discussed in Chapter 5), and some argue that it would be better to wait to avoid being offered second-class membership. Views in Bulgaria are unclear and there seems to be little discussion of this issue; while in opposition, the Union of Democratic Forces (UDF) seemed to have quite unrealistic expectations of joining fairly rapidly (Shikova and Nikolov 1997), but expectations are changing as a result of the Commission's opinion and better understanding of the problems now that the party is in office.

It is not clear how differentiation at the start of negotiations will affect the political situations in those countries excluded from them. The impact will depend partly on how fast those outside are approaching membership and partly on how governments handle the issue. So far the domestic political impact of the NATO decisions and Commission recommendations has not been dramatic. But if countries appear to be becoming excluded from the process despite reform efforts, there could be more of a domestic backlash.

Approaches to managing the domestic political impact of differentiation vary across the five countries not recommended to start negotiations. In Slovakia, Prime Minister Vladimir Meciar already shows signs of wanting to muddy the waters, confusing the question of whether Slovakia is ready to start negotiations by criticizing EU views on his government's actions. The aim seems to be that his attendance at a 'champagne and chandeliers' opening conference would show that he is accepted among other European leaders, while he continues to proclaim to the EU that Slovakia is nearly ready to start negotiations. However, it is uncertain whether this would be enough to overcome the fact that Slovakia was not actually beginning negotiations, even if the issue were not effectively exploited by the opposition parties in the short term.

The Latvian and Lithuanian governments have adopted a strategy of presenting more material and criticizing the recommendations, and they have a strong case to join negotiations in the next few years, given the system of annual reviews proposed by the Commission. Romania and Bulgaria have not experienced any immediately destabilizing effects, but fairly wide-ranging disappointment has emerged. For Romania, the EU's decision follows on quickly from NATO's rejection; the combination of the two decisions could make it more difficult for the government as it pushes through painful reforms. For Bulgaria, the EU has been particularly important as a motivating factor for reforms, and thus the EU's decision on negotiations has the worrying potential to destabilize the government's efforts. However, the framework provided by the Accession Partnerships and the European Conference could help to reduce the sense of exclusion. For both countries, the need to respond to the *avis* and agree to Accession Partnerships after the Luxembourg European Council presents difficult decisions on priorities when faced with taking on the *acquis* and dealing with immediate economic problems at the same time.

Public opinion

Public opinion on EU accession is important in establishing the legitimacy of the process, particularly given that many CEE countries will hold referenda on membership. So far it has been generally supportive of joining, but there are variations across the ten countries and there have been some changes since the early years of transition. Here we will look at the main evidence for broad trends in public opinion.[2]

Public support is now lower than in the early years of transition, but it has recently recovered somewhat in most countries apart from the Baltic states. At the most general level of whether or not voters would support EU accession in a referendum, on average two-thirds of those who have the right to vote would vote 'yes' (see Figure 6.1). However, this average conceals a major gap between the two most enthusiastic countries, Romania and Poland, which show 80% and 70% support respectively, and the rest. In the other eight countries, those who would vote for EU membership accounted for less than half of the total, ranging from 49% in Bulgaria down to 29% in Estonia. Around another quarter to a third of respondents in Slovakia, the Czech Republic and the Baltic states were undecided. The number of those who would vote against accession was relatively small, ranging from 17% in Estonia down to 2% in Romania.

[2] In the interest of comparability across countries and time, the following discussion draws principally on the surveys of public opinion in the EU and CEE conducted by Eurobarometer (the survey research unit of the European Commission) since 1989, although there is some comparison with national opinion polls. The latest *Central and Eastern Eurobarometer* report is based on interviews conducted in November 1996.

Figure 6.1: Referendum on EU membership in candidate countries

Q: If there were to be a referendum tomorrow on the question of our country's membership of the EU, would you personally vote for or against membership?

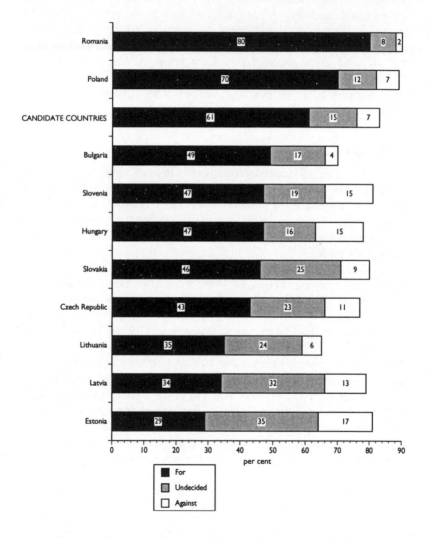

Source: European Commission, *Central and European Eurobarometer* No. 7.

Table 6.1: Trends in positive views[a] of the EU, 1990–96 (%)

	1990	1991	1992	1993	1994	1995	1996
Romania	–	52	55	45	51	50	65
Poland	46	49	48	37	42	46	58
Bulgaria	47	46	51	42	37	27	42
Slovenia	–	–	45	30	37	35	35
Slovakia	43	37	35	44	37	31	34
Hungary	51	42	34	36	32	30	33
Czech Republic	49	46	45	37	34	36	33
Latvia	–	45	40	40	35	35	26
Estonia	–	38	32	31	29	30	24
Lithuania	–	51	43	45	34	23	22

[a] Remaining percentage share are neutral, negative or 'don't know'.
Source: Central and Eastern Eurobarometer No. 7.

These differences in aggregate views reflect different geo-political situations and historical experiences, although the aggregate level of these data makes it difficult to draw out reliably specific factors for each country. Nevertheless, one evident trend is that levels of positive support are lower in the newly independent countries and higher in the already established states (with the possible exception of Hungary); this probably reflects at least in part the experience of having left a federation recently.

The data shown in Figure 6.1 are particularly important given that most of the CEE countries are likely to have a referendum on accession. Opinion will change and opposition could grow, particularly during a set of long and difficult negotiations, but on current trends it is unlikely that any of the applicants would end up with a rejection of EU membership in a referendum. All of these poll findings have to be considered against a background of quite limited knowledge of and interest in a European Union that is still seen as quite remote, as evidenced in previous *Central and Eastern Eurobarometer* reports and those by the University of Strathclyde (see Rose and Haerpfer 1995). Moreover, a number of factors could change in the years preceding accession, most importantly how successfully transition proceeds and how well the EU handles its own preparations for enlargement.

Reasons given why people would vote for or against EU membership are primarily general ones reflecting experiences of transition so far; those in favour of membership cite expectations of benefits from access-ion: general progress thanks to EU help (32%), economic improvement or market opening (26%) and higher living standards (15%). Reasons for opposition to EU membership are less distinct; the main reasons given are that the EU will aggravate the economic crisis, is too expensive or is of no benefit (5%), while a small number are afraid of loss of identity or independence (2%). Overall, economic reasons seem to be much more important than political ones, a conclusion borne out by national polls (Tamási 1997, and Shikova and Nikolov 1997).

More detail on attitudes can be found in response to questions about the image of the EU. On average, nearly half saw the EU's image as positive, a further third as neutral, and a small number as negative (see Figure 6.2). Trends in individual countries over the past six years have varied considerably (see Table 6.1). Romania, Poland and Bulgaria have the highest level of positive *avis* and have also shown the most pronounced rise between 1995 and 1996; indeed, Romania is the only country to have a higher level of positive views now than in 1991, when the level was 52%. There was also an increase of 7% in the number of positive views in the Czech Republic over 1995, although this rise follows five years of decline, from 49% in 1990 down to 26% in 1995. National opinion polls also suggest that there has been some recovery in support for joining (see Bohatá and Mládek 1997).

Views in Slovenia, Hungary and Slovakia have remained relatively stable over the past three or four years. In the Baltic states, however, there has been a marked deterioration in the image of the EU since 1991, with positive views falling by 14 percentage points in Estonia, 19 in Latvia and 27 in Lithuania. This decline in positive views has been accompanied by a large rise in neutral views, with the level of negative views still low. However, the trend in the Baltic states stands in contrast to those in most of the other applicant countries, where initially very high levels of positive images declined and then later recovered to some extent; in all of the countries, there remains disappointment at the EU not being more welcoming and at the difficulties of transition.

At the end of 1996 *Central and Eastern Eurobarometer* also canvassed 'decision-makers and opinion-formers'. This group generally has a more positive image of the EU than does the wider public: on average, 80% has a positive view, with only 14% neutral and 3% negative, whereas the average for the general public is only half positive. Parliamentarians are on average 89% positive about the EU's aims and activities, political parties and journalists slightly less, while central government and the private sector are both three-quarters positive. However, the views of Czech, Estonian and Latvian decision-makers are at the bottom of the range, with between two-thirds and a half having positive images; this

Figure 6.2: Impressions of the aims and activities of the EU, 1996

Q: As you know, 15 states of 'western' Europe together form the 'European Union'. Would you say that your impressions of the aims and activities of the European Union are generally positive, neutral or negative?

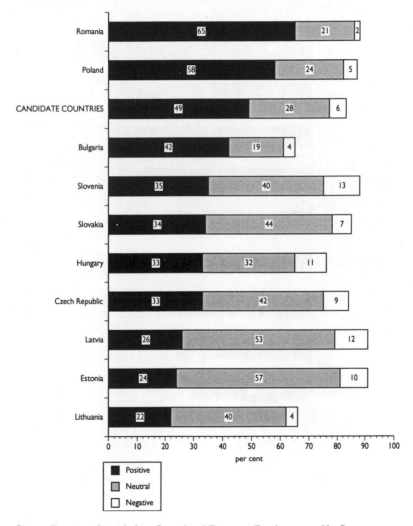

Source: European Commission, *Central and European Eurobarometer* No. 7.

85

Figure 6.3: Who might win or lose as ties with the EU become closer?

Q: Do you think the following are likely to benefit or lose out in (our country) as ties between (our country) and the European Union increase? What do you think will happen to … :

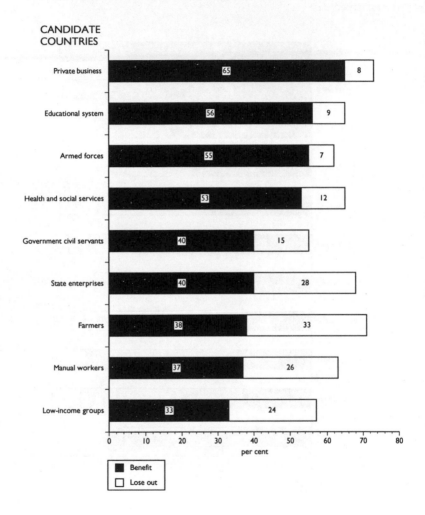

Source: European Commission, *Central and European Eurobarometer* No. 7.

difference is in line with the lower level of positive images of the EU among the public in these countries (although the level of positive images was much higher for this group than for the public).

When asked about the orientation of the post-communist countries, people are more strongly in favour of the EU than of the United States, Russia or the other CEE countries. On average, 40% of CEE inhabitants see their country's future as most closely tied up with the EU. In Romania, where a similar number saw the USA as more important in 1995, there was a 10 percentage point increase in favour of the EU by November 1996. In Hungary and Poland a significant number spontaneously replied that Germany was most important to their future. The largest number of people seeing Russia as most important are found in the Baltic countries and Bulgaria. These views may result as much from a feeling of threat from Russia as from a sense of opportunity, and the replies in the Baltic states may be connected to their large Russian minority populations; it is interesting to note that there have been considerable gains for Russia in Latvia since 1994. In both Latvia and Estonia, a significant part of the population is disenfranchised through being non-citizens; this may account for some of the difference between political debates and opinion polls on whether the EU or Russia is most important in foreign policy, although other factors almost certainly come into play here too.

Despite the overall support for a westward orientation, the public in CEE seems more doubtful about who benefits from relations with the EU. On average, by far the largest number of people feel that their country and the EU benefit equally from relations (44%). These data suggest that the public appreciate that joining the EU might not be advantageous to their country in every respect, and yet they support accession nonetheless because of the overall benefits.

When asked who might win or lose from closer ties with the EU, on average 65% think that private business would gain, and more than half think the educational system, the armed forces and health and social services would gain (see Figure 6.3). State enterprises, farmers, manual workers and low-income groups are most often expected to lose out. The countries where there was most concern that farmers might lose out are Slovenia, the Czech Republic, Estonia, Latvia and Poland, and overall respondents in the candidate countries are divided as to whether or not farmers will benefit (38% yes and 33% no).

Support for EU accession across the CEE-10 is generally much higher than support for joining NATO across these countries. Romania and

Poland are again far in the lead in terms of support (with 76% and 65% saying they would vote 'yes' to NATO), with all the others showing between 39% and 27% support. The largest number of those undecided how to vote (roughly a third of respondents) was found in the Baltic states, whose membership of NATO is most strongly opposed by Russia, and in Slovakia.

Average support for NATO membership was lower than for joining the EU, with 53% saying they would vote for membership, 17% undecided and 10% saying they would vote against. However, national polls taken since the Madrid decision in July 1997 to invite Poland, Hungary and the Czech Republic to join indicate an increase in public support for membership in those countries, and the Hungarian referendum in November 1997 produced a 'yes' vote of 85%. In the Eurobarometer survey, by far the most important reason given for voting decisions was that NATO would guarantee security and stability in the region (49% of responses); of the very few negative reasons given, 7% opposed NATO membership because they favoured neutrality. Underlying these views is the tendency for NATO to be seen in CEE as a relic of the Cold War in a way that the EU is not.

Conclusions

Political debate in CEE is still concerned mostly with the general principle of joining the EU rather than the implications of membership for specific policy areas or societal groups. The very high degree of consensus among political actors and commentators suggests that changes in government are unlikely to result in major changes on EU policy, although the contrasting views on many domestic policy issues between political parties could have an impact on attitudes towards some aspects of relations with the EU and the speed with which countries move towards meeting EU requirements.

This general consensus can be expected to change as knowledge increases about what the EU is and how membership will affect different groups of people in CEE. Already the Commission's opinions have provoked more debate in the press about accession in CEE, and treatment of the applicants in negotiations could make a difference as issues such as barriers to the movement of people, trade and the size of transfers come under discussion. Changes in the outlook for the timing of accessions will start to impinge too, bringing greater awareness of the variables involved in the process of enlargement. Moreover, these factors will interact with political and economic developments in the different countries over the years leading up to accession.

In contrast to the elite consensus across CEE, public opinion varies across the ten countries. Given the relatively low levels of support in some countries already, a 'yes' vote in referenda on EU membership cannot be guaranteed in all ten countries, although on current trends this is the most likely outcome; growing awareness of the fact that all the CEE members will be net recipients from the budget is likely to encourage support as awareness of this factor grows. Public opinion on who is likely to gain or lose from closer ties provides some pointers for the groups whose causes could be taken up by political parties; however, it is not clear when, how and if disadvantages of EU membership will be perceived by voters in various CEE countries. Different issues are likely to have salience in the different countries: agriculture, borders, minorities, relations with Russia and transfers do not have the same resonance in each.

During the process of negotiations, political debates and party stances can be expected to develop as understanding of the EU and the implications of membership grows in CEE. These debates will respond to the negotiations, particularly as sensitive issues arise and the full extent of EU requirements becomes clearer, but they will also affect negotiating stances themselves. This dual impact has the potential to complicate the process of negotiations, as has happened in previous enlargements, but it will also help to define CEE preferences as these countries become member states.

Chapter 7

Readying the EU for enlargement

Introduction

Enlargement to encompass 26 or more member states will fundamentally change the nature and functioning of the EU. The immediate impact of the first accessions will be felt primarily through their effect on policies and institutions. These two broad areas are increasingly a focus of debate within the current EU-15, and enlargement has the potential to exacerbate many of the tensions already present in the Union. The accession of ten relatively poor CEE countries, even in a series of smaller accessions with long transitional periods, will inevitably affect both Community finances and the way the Union works. As already indicated, in absorbing all ten countries, the EU would add 28% to its population but only 4%[1] to its GDP, and average per capita GDP in the CEE-10 is only one-third of the average EU level.[2] The functioning of EU institutions and their ability to achieve central policy goals will be affected by the scale of the enterprise, and the fact that the process of adjustment is likely to be gradual raises questions about whether the EU will be able to ensure that the result is a cohesive and effective Union.

EU policies and the budget

The budget debate
Over the past 40 years, the EC/EU has developed a wide range of policies to which each new member has had to adapt. In previous enlargements,

[1] At current market prices.
[2] On a purchasing power parity (PPP) basis.

the Community budget has been used to counterbalance the costs of adaptation for new members by offering them fiscal transfers to aid specific parts of their integration with existing member states. Even when net contributors have joined (as with the EFTA accessions of 1995), funds have been made available to deal with particularly sensitive adaptations of national policy. Despite this history, however, the mood in the Union is firmly against the idea of any substantial increase in the budget as a percentage of EU GNP to help bring new CEE members into EU policies or to encourage economic convergence between East and West. Indeed, a considerable proportion of the debate about eastward enlargement has so far been taken up with discussion of its potential costs in budgetary terms.

The two main components of the budget are the CAP and the Structural and Cohesion Funds, which together account for around 80% of total expenditure. The prospect of major cuts to pay for increased transfers to the East would provoke opposition from two of the most powerful lobbying groups in the EU: farmers and the recipients of regional aid. In Agenda 2000 the Commission has presented its proposals for budgetary and policy reform in the context of enlargement. It aims to avoid backlash from the lobbies by limiting the overall financial impact of its proposals. Nonetheless, member states have differing interests in budget and policy reform, many of which are highly politically sensitive. Without a relatively swift solution to the budgetary problem posed by the costs of enlargement, there is a danger that financial concerns will lead to a deliberate slowing of the enlargement process.

The key to finding an acceptable solution to the policy challenges raised by CEE accessions is an overall deal on the future of the budget which ensures the support of all EU member states for enlargement and overrides the objections of current sectoral and regional recipients of major EU funds. After all, every member state will have a veto over the accession treaties and every legislature will have to ratify them, so there are numerous opportunities for budgetary lobbies to disrupt the process.

There are essentially three competing pressures on the process of budgetary reform:

(1) *Maintaining budget discipline* In the climate of fiscal austerity created by the EMU criteria, the main net contributors are determined to ensure that the budget remains within its current ceiling as a percentage of EU GNP; indeed, Germany and the Netherlands are demanding a reduction in their current contributions.

(2) *Reassuring current beneficiaries* The net recipients of the Structural and Cohesion Funds, led by Spain, and farmers across the EU, could try to block the accessions if major cuts in transfers are threatened. Even Ireland, which is widely expected to graduate out of the Cohesion Fund owing to its economic success, has argued that this should be only a gradual process.

(3) *Ensuring that the CEE countries are not made second-class members of the EU by being excluded from its central policies* The principle of equal treatment between member states is a central feature of EU membership, and imposing very long transitional conditions on the CEE countries would create a multi-tier EU even in the medium run.

The first requirement is related to the second because several of the large net contributors also face strong domestic lobbying to continue support to their farmers or to particular regions. The political pressures on Germany and Italy are especially problematic in this respect; the Mezzogiorno receives significant transfers from the EU budget that Rome does not want to see reduced. Germany is in the contradictory position of wanting to reduce its budget contribution but also to limit reforms because Bonn is under pressure to resist cuts in payments to farmers and to maintain regional aids, especially to the eastern *Länder*. Farming lobbies across the EU have much greater political clout than their importance in GDP and employment might seem to warrant, and these cross-cutting issues complicate member states' negotiating positions on the budget. Wider political considerations enter too; in particular, little change is expected in the German position until after its general election in the autumn of 1998. Even then, getting the crucial German agreement on budgetary and policy reform will be difficult, especially on the CAP.

The Commission's budget proposals The Commission aims to square the circle of competing pressures by proposing that the budget run from 2000 to 2006 with no increase in the 1999 expenditure ceiling of 1.27% of EU GNP, but assuming that economic expansion will allow the absolute size of the budget to increase. Provided there is growth of 2.5% for the EU and 4% for the CEE countries, the Commission calculates that by 2006 there will be slightly more than 20bn ECU (at 1997 prices) in additional resources available. The Commission also assumes that the first round of accession will not occur before 2002, and that the new members will by then have transitional arrangements (especially for extending the CAP), so the increase in expenditure for enlargement will be gradual.

This framework allows the Commission to pencil in an absolute increase in expenditure on the CAP and a small reduction in regional aid for the EU-15, as well as an allocation of around 75bn ECU for the applicant countries. The current member states would thus see an overall increase in net receipts from the budget during the period 2000–2006. Expenditure on some policies would be reduced, but exactly where the axe might fall is left uncertain. Despite some accessions occurring during this period, net contributors would be able to keep the 1.27% ceiling sacrosanct. The Commission proposes maintaining the current system for financing the budget over the next financial perspective, with a fundamental reform of the arrangements if and when the EU requires an increase in the overall ceiling.

Will this compromise satisfy all the interests in the current EU? The outcome depends on several factors:

- how the distribution of transfers changes. As is explained below, the next financial perspective will see the start of major reforms in the way the CAP and regional aid funds operate, which will be opposed by many current recipients. CAP reform looks likely to be the most difficult element to resolve.
- whether the Commission's assumptions are realized, depending particularly on economic growth and the effective operation of new policy structures.
- whether all the member states accept the proposals as fair. Net recipients and contributors are already arguing that the others should pay more for enlargement; for example, northern member states are likely to argue that the proportion of the budget taken by the Structural Funds is too high, while southern ones may advocate an overall increase in the size of the budget to cope with enlargement, implying that contributions should increase.

The budget and enlargement Under the Commission's growth assumptions, the total EU budget for 2000–2006 would be 745.5bn ECU, of which the ten CEE applicants would receive 74.8 bn ECU; this allocation for CEE is just over 10% of the budget and a thousandth (0.127%) of EU GDP. Even by 2006, the ten applicants together will only account for 16% of the EU budget and the five backmarkers will account for 2.6%. These are small amounts to allocate for such a momentous step and to so many countries, but they will still be controversial among member states.

The new acceding members will not in the initial years get the same levels of support as the old member states. This discrepancy in levels of support suggests that, once the new members join, they will have a strong interest in arguing for higher transfers and equality of treatment. Budget negotiations in future years could be more difficult than the current round. Although countries such as Poland and Spain have opposing viewpoints at present, once Poland joins the EU they will have a common interest in arguing for further transfers.

Table 7.1 sets out the Commission's proposed allocations to the ten applicants. The Commission uses the working assumption that the five countries it recommends for starting negotiations will actually join in 2002. Between 2002 and 2006, the acceding countries would receive 53.8bn ECU, consisting of 38bn ECU from the Structural Funds and 15.8bn ECU from the CAP and other agricultural support. In the pre-

Table 7.1: The Commission's budget proposals for the CEE-10, 2000–2006

	ECU (1997 prices)							
	2000	2001	2002	2003	2004	2005	2006	Total
Five front-runners[a]								
Pre-accession aid								
Agriculture	0.3	0.3	–	–	–	–	–	0.6
Phare	0.9	0.9	–	–	–	–	–	1.8
Structural operations	0.6	0.6	–	–	–	–	–	1.2
Transfers after accession[b]								
Structural Funds	–	–	3.6	5.6	7.6	9.6	11.6	38.0
Agriculture	–	–	1.5	1.9	2.4	2.9	3.3	12.0
Other internal policies	–	–	0.7	0.7	0.8	0.8	0.8	3.8
Total first five	1.8	1.8	5.8	8.2	10.8	13.3	15.7	57.4
Five backmarkers[c]								
Pre-accession aid								
Agriculture	0.2	0.2	0.5	0.5	0.5	0.5	0.5	2.9
Phare	0.6	0.6	1.5	1.5	1.5	1.5	1.5	8.7
Structural operations	0.4	0.4	1.0	1.0	1.0	1.0	1.0	5.8
Total second five	1.2	1.2	3.0	3.0	3.0	3.0	3.0	17.4
Total CEE-10	3.0	3.0	8.8	11.2	13.8	16.3	18.7	74.8

[a] Czech Republic, Estonia, Hungary, Poland and Slovenia.
[b] Agenda 2000 makes a 'technical working assumption' that five CEE countries plus Cyprus join in 2002.
[c] Bulgaria, Latvia, Lithuania, Romania and Slovakia.
Source: CEC (1997).

accession phase, the five front-runners would get 3.6bn ECU for 2000–2001 from Phare, the Structural Funds and agricultural support. Overall, they would receive 57.4bn ECU.

For all the applicants, the Commission proposes total expenditure over the period 2000–2006 of 21bn ECU on pre-accession aid, comprising 10.5bn ECU from Phare, 7bn ECU from the Structural Funds, and 3.5bn ECU of support for agricultural reform.[3] The five that would remain outside the EU would receive 17.4bn ECU, which is 23% of the budget allocation to the CEE-10, while the five front-runners would get 77%. Although the Commission proposes transferring the pre-accession funds to the lagging five once the front-runners have become members, the five backmarkers will still be receiving substantially less than the new member states, threatening to widen the gap between the two groups. Some member states are also likely to oppose giving the five backmarkers these additional pre-accession funds.

Over the proposed seven-year period, the five front-runners will get over 900 ECU per head (130 ECU per head each year) while the five backmarkers will get under 410 ECU per head (58 ECU per head each year). Thus, the front five will get twice as much as the lagging five, although even the front-runners will get substantially less than the current EU net recipients, particularly the cohesion countries. This funding gap casts serious doubt on the EU's commitment to solidarity and convergence; moreover, it focuses most assistance on the five front-runners, leaving the five lagging countries coping not only with the political impact of perceived exclusion, but also with the actual fact of demonstrably smaller levels of financial assistance. The EU's political message is that the lagging five are part of the whole process and should not feel excluded; if this message is to be accepted as genuine, the distribution of financial resources will have to be reconsidered.

Agriculture

The Common Agricultural Policy is the complex regime that governs state support for agriculture in the EU. Accession of new members to the EU without including the CAP would mean leaving a traditionally central policy out of the *acquis communautaire*, effectively creating a form of second-class membership. Equally, however, a 'big bang' reform of the CAP, to be implemented in advance of a first enlargement early in the

---

[3] The Luxembourg European Council agreed to a European Commission proposal for a 'catch-up facility', but the amounts involved seem unlikely to be large.

next century, seems unlikely given political circumstances in the EU. Historically a core EU policy, the CAP retains a political significance well beyond the role of agriculture in the EU economy that has enabled it to survive many previous attempts at reform. However, enlargement is not the only issue involved in the future of the CAP. Reforms in 1992 lessened the immediate pressures on the policy, but further changes will be stimulated by the next round of multilateral trade talks starting in 1999.

The CAP currently accounts for nearly half of the EU budget: it will cost just under 40bn ECU in 1999. Extending the policy in its present form to new CEE members with larger and less efficient agricultural sectors would have major financial implications, although these are difficult to calculate because of uncertainties about potential agricultural output in the CEE countries. The importance of agriculture varies widely across the CEE economies (as shown in Table 7.2); there are particularly striking differences between the significant role the sector plays in Polish and Romanian employment against its relatively minor role in the Czech Republic, Slovakia and Slovenia. Overall, agriculture accounts for a considerably higher proportion of GDP and employment in CEE than is the case in the EU. The traditional justifications used for the CAP – especially the role of farmers in society and the need for an integrated rural policy – thus apply with additional force to CEE. For most CEE countries, a rapid decline in the size of the agricultural sector would cause urbanization and unemployment on a scale that transition economies could not cope with; however, in the medium run substantial restructuring of the sector is inevitable in the face of falling levels of subsidies and protection.

Market conditions in the CEE agricultural and food sectors are significantly different from those prevailing in the EU. In general, prices are only 40–80% of EU levels (CEC 1995) owing to high support prices under the CAP and the lower quality relative to EU agricultural products, although the latter varies across the region. Levels of protection are also much lower, ranging from about 20% in Poland, Hungary and the Czech Republic down to 1% in Latvia. Productivity levels are generally considerably lower, particularly since the falls experienced in the early years of transition (Hartmann 1996), and all except Hungary are net food importers from the EU (CEC 1995).

The potential increase in CEE agricultural output seems to be considerable in the long run, particularly if labour productivity rises rapidly. Much depends on how quickly functioning land markets can develop, how the farm sector can reorganize itself to strengthen the

Table 7.2: Relative importance of agriculture in the CEE-10 and EU-15, 1995

	Agricultural production as % of GDP	Employment in agriculture as % of total
Czech Republic	5.2	6.3
Hungary	6.2	8.0
Poland	7.6	26.9
Slovakia	6.3	9.7
Slovenia	5.0	7.1
Bulgaria	13.9	23.2
Romania	20.5	34.4
Estonia	8.1	13.1
Latvia	9.9	18.5
Lithuania	9.3	23.8
CEE-10 total	8.6	22.5
EU-15 total	2.4[a]	5.3

[a] Figure for 1994.
Source: CEC (1997), Vol. II, p. 68.

supply chain from farms to processing and distribution, and the speed at which new technology is introduced into the CEE economies. The Commission expects land reform and restructuring of the food supply chain to take at least until 2000, while farm structures will evolve more slowly owing to limitations on investment (CEC 1995). The effect of changes in output levels on CEE agricultural exports depends on a range of factors, chiefly quality improvements, input prices and availability, and the development of the food processing industry (Hartmann 1996), as well as whether there is further liberalization of agricultural trade.

The impact on the EU budget of extending the current CAP is difficult to calculate and the various estimates made so far are not directly comparable because they are based on a variety of models, supply projections and assumptions of changes to the CAP. However, the overall range seems to be an increase of 30–50% over the cost of the current CAP for the EU-15 (House of Lords 1996). In addition to the budgetary implications, full extension of the CAP may in the long run be detrimental to CEE agriculture because the traditional priorities of the CAP regime are arguably inappropriate to a sector whose principal needs are better access to capital, a restructuring of productive capacity and the improvement of downstream operations. CEE farmers are already adjusting to world markets more rapidly than their EU counterparts, so a full extension of the current CAP would run counter to the general thrust of liberalization efforts and market-oriented reforms in CEE.

Reform in the context of enlargement Enlargement is not the only factor forcing the EU towards changing the CAP. For most of its history, the CAP has been under pressure for reform, primarily to reduce costs. The 1992 MacSharry reforms began to decouple support to farmers from production, but this remains incomplete and prices remain well above world prices. There is also increasing attention in the EU to the need to address the environmental and public health problems caused by intensive farming, particularly because of the BSE (bovine spongiform encephalitis) epidemic and the ensuing political crisis. External pressures on the CAP will grow as a result of the next WTO round of world trade liberalization; follow-up negotiations in agriculture are due to start in 1999 to build on the GATT Uruguay Round of 1993. The EU's trading partners are likely to press for further reductions in price support, increased access to EU markets and further reductions in export subsidies; at the same time, a number of member states (particularly France) would like to improve access for their agricultural exports. Although negotiations could be lengthy, they are ultimately likely to cause profound changes to the CAP.

The Commission's approach to reform (as outlined in Agenda 2000) is to continue the general thrust of the MacSharry reforms by reducing guaranteed prices and export subsidies, while increasing direct aid to farmers and decoupling it from production volume. Aid would thus be focused on increasing farmers' incomes, but without encouraging them to produce more, and the market distortions created by price-fixing would be reduced. Overall, the Commission proposes reducing the support prices for beef, cereals and milk by 30%, 20% and 10% respectively, but there would be no time limit on compensatory payments for the price cuts. There would also be additional funds available for new rural development measures and fisheries.

The total budget available for the EU-15 would be 50bn ECU by 2006, with 4.5 bn ECU for new member states and those still receiving pre-accession aid. The agricultural policy guideline would be 59.2bn ECU, leaving a substantial margin (4.7bn ECU) for member states to review in 2005; this surplus could be used to cover additional expenditure resulting from market uncertainties or to introduce measures such as continuing reform of the CAP and ending transitional periods for new members.[4]

[4] All figures are in 1997 prices.

In practice, it is likely to be difficult to achieve the Commission's reform proposals for the EU-15, partly because of the CAP's very complexity, which makes reform outcomes uncertain in financial terms, but mostly because of opposition from the powerful farming lobbies in key member states. The UK and Sweden are arguing for more radical reform than that proposed in Agenda 2000, but the other member states would like to see the Commission's proposals cut back to varying extents. Germany's position will be critical to getting a deal, and its farming lobby is already arguing that no reform is needed. Change thus looks likely to be slow and incremental, and ultimately the WTO negotiations may prove a greater stimulus to reform than enlargement.

The Commission allocates the CEE countries less than 10% of that available for the EU-15 by 2006; it is intended to be used for reorganizing the agricultural sector rather than introducing the price-support mechanisms traditionally provided by the CAP in the EU. To start with, pre-accession aid of 500 million ECU a year for all ten is designated for farm modernization and improving distribution in the sector. After the first accessions, those still outside the EU would receive all the 500 million ECU, increasing their receipts of assistance. Meanwhile, the new members, assumed to join in 2002, would receive CAP funds for market organization and modernization on a rising scale from the year of accession to the end of the financial perspective; the total over the period would be 12bn ECU. There is little expectation that further liberalization of agricultural trade between the EU and CEE will occur prior to accession, despite the importance attached to this issue by CEE. Given the much larger levels of assistance that the five front-runners will receive relative to the five second-wave countries, opening agricultural markets to the second wave will be very important both in assisting transition and in demonstrating genuine commitment to these countries.

Regional funds
The Structural and Cohesion Funds are intended to narrow economic disparities across EU member states, and so they might be expected to play a central role when much poorer economies join. However, there is little indication that the CEE countries will be allocated funds on the same criteria as those used for poorer regions and countries among the existing member states.

The Structural Funds are currently divided into six regional policy objectives; Objective 1, which accounts for 70% of the total funds, goes only to regions where GDP per head is below 75% of the EU average.

Table 7.3: Estimates of the cost of extending the Structural Funds to CEE

	bn ECU
CEE-6[a] (Baldwin 1994)	26.0
CEE-6[a] (UK government 1995)[b]	31.5
CEE-10 (Danish Economic Ministry 1996)[c]	14–20
CEE-10 (CEC 1995)[d]	38

[a] CEE-6 are Bulgaria, Czech Republic, Hungary, Poland, Romania and Slovakia.
[b] From a DTI paper distributed in 1995.
[c] Report on the economic implications of enlargement published by Marianne Jelved, Danish Minster for Economic Affairs, 1 February 1996.
[d] Unofficial Commission estimate reported in the *Financial Times*, 23 October 1995.

Eligibility for the Cohesion Fund is restricted to member states with a per capita GDP of less than 90% of the EU average (Greece, Ireland, Portugal and Spain). The funds' wide range of policy objectives (from industrial decline to unemployment, rural development, environmental protection and infrastructure investment) is highly relevant to the needs of economies in transition. There would be no shortage of uses for the funds given the CEE countries' clear need for help with major problems such as environmental clean-up and improvement of infrastructure; however, other traditional EU priorities such as aid for regions in industrial decline could conflict with the economic transition policies so far adopted by CEE governments.

Cost estimates of extending the Structural and Cohesion Funds on their current basis to the CEE-10 suggest a doubling of the existing level (see Table 7.3). A common method for estimating the costs of extending the Structural Funds is to apply the amount per head received by Greece and Portugal, using either current figures or projected figures for 1999 (see e.g. Brenton and Gros 1993, CEC 1993). In all of the CEE-10 countries, GDP per head is below that of Greece and Portugal, which have the lowest levels in the current EU. The accession of these countries would lower the EU's average GDP per head by 16%, with the implication that many current recipients (cohesion countries and regions of other EU member states) would no longer qualify for aid, particularly under Objective 1 of the Structural Funds.

Table 7.4 sets out an estimate of the costs of extending the Structural Funds on the assumption that the CEE-10 receive assistance at the rate of 400 ECU per head, which is the estimated amount for Greece and Portugal in 1999 (CEC 1993). This gives a total of 42.12bn ECU for the

Table 7.4: Calculation of the cost of extending the Structural Funds to CEE

	Structural fund estimates at 400 ECU per capita (bn ECU)	Structural fund estimates as % of GDP [a]	Structural fund estimates with 4% of GDP limit (bn ECU)
Poland	15.44	17.1	3.60
Romania	9.08	33.2	1.09
Czech Republic	4.12	11.4	1.44
Hungary	4.08	12.2	1.33
Bulgaria	3.36	33.9	0.39
Slovakia	2.16	16.2	0.53
Lithuania	1.48	42.2	0.14
Latvia	1.00	29.4	0.13
Slovenia	0.80	5.6	0.56
Estonia	0.60	21.4	0.11
Total CEE	42.12		9.36

[a] Calculation based on GDP at market prices.
Source: own calculations based on CEC (1997).

CEE-10, compared with a total of 28.4bn ECU for the EU-15 in 1999.

It has been argued that, without reform, the Structural Funds would provide the CEE countries with such high levels of assistance that, first, they would find it difficult to provide matching funds and, secondly, they would have serious absorption problems. As is shown in the second column of Table 7.4, the Structural Funds would represent amounts ranging from nearly 6% of Slovenia's GDP to 42% of Lithuania's.

The Commission has proposed that the Structural Funds be reformed to focus on a smaller proportion of the EU's population and on a smaller number of objectives, but most of the money would still go to existing member states rather than new members. Of the total allocation of 275bn ECU proposed for 2000–2006, 230bn ECU would be for the EU-15 and only 45bn ECU for the CEE-10 (at 1997 prices). Two-thirds of the Structural Funds budget for current member states would be allocated to Objective 1 regions, with the regions that move above the threshold (of 75% of average GDP per head) only gradually being phased out of these arrangements. The remaining third of the total would be concentrated on a smaller proportion of the EU population and would be slightly decreased over the financial perspective. However, EU-15 regions would also get new rural development accompanying measures under the CAP budget. Moreover, eligibility for the Cohesion Fund will not be reviewed until 2003, with a total allocation of 20bn ECU for the whole period. These proposals would thus prevent any current recipient of regional aid from being cut off from the funds immediately.

For the CEE-10, the Commission proposes an overall Structural Funds allocation of 45bn ECU, of which 7bn ECU (1bn ECU per annum) would be pre-accession aid (in addition to Phare aid of 1.5bn ECU a year); the five front-runners would then get 38bn ECU from 2002 assuming they become new member states then. According to this proposal, once the first accessions have taken place, the five second-wave countries will receive the 1bn ECU that was previously allocated to all ten. The second-wave group will therefore get higher absolute amounts after the first accessions, but a very large gap will open up between their levels of assistance and that of the five new members; from 2002 to 2006 the new members will receive 38bn ECU, while the five back-markers will get only 5bn ECU. On an annual per capita basis, this is equivalent to the front-runner group receiving about 120 ECU per head (rising to about 185 per head in 2006) and the lagging group receiving about 23 ECU per head (or almost 60 ECU per head including Phare) in 2002–2006.

Even the amount received by the front-runners is well under half the transfers to Greece and Portugal in 1999 of 400 ECU per head. This is partly due to the Commission's assumption that there will be transitional periods before new members join the regional aid funds, but it is also because Agenda 2000 proposes moving away from per capita comparisons between countries and towards introducing an overall ceiling of 4% of GNP on Structural Funds receipts.

This formula quite neatly allows the Commission to reduce substantially the costs of extending the Structural Funds to CEE (as shown in the last column of Table 7.4) and it deals with potential absorption problems for the CEE countries; however, it moves away from the principle of equality of treatment between member states. Poorer countries will receive less per head than richer countries. Moreover, the ceiling will have the perverse effect of providing more assistance to the higher-income CEE countries, and increasing transfers to them as they become richer. There is a strong argument that the CEE countries' greatest need for transfers is in the early years, when they face the worst economic problems and their national budgets are most constrained. The Commission's proposals might help to solve the sensitive questions of Structural Funds reform and allocations to the applicants, but at the cost of important principles of solidarity and cohesion. This approach also misses the key aim of promoting convergence and catch-up in levels of economic development across the enlarged EU.

Institutional reform: will the enlarged EU work?

Enlargement of the EU to 26 or more members raises difficult questions about the future functioning of the EU's institutions. Strains have already emerged as the EU has expanded to 15 members. Yet, while it is widely accepted that institutional change is necessary for enlargement, there is less agreement on the nature, extent and timing of these changes among member states. The Intergovernmental Conference (IGC) that concluded at Amsterdam in June 1997 failed to resolve any of these issues.

The principal focus of concerns about enlargement and institutional functioning is the question of efficient operating procedures and decision-making; proposals to reform procedures, however, also need to take into account issues of democracy and legitimacy. After all, efficiency and democracy do not always pull in the same direction. The discussion so far has also focused on reforming procedures within the existing structures and policies of the EU; redefining the *acquis communautaire* has been an almost taboo subject. While there has been substantial discussion about flexibility for future policies, amendment of the existing *acquis* to accommodate enlargement has received little attention.

Although the IGC was billed as the conference that would make the changes necessary for enlargement and open the path to negotiations, the Amsterdam summit failed to agree on even small, initial reforms. It was never to be expected that the IGC would seriously address the question of how a 26-member-state EU would function, given political time-horizons and the fact that the EU will not reach this size for many years. But it was expected that some of the initial steps would be taken, especially since the EU had put off publishing *avis* on the applications and taking a decision on opening negotiations until the IGC had been successfully concluded.

The importance of the failure of Amsterdam lies first in its public demonstration of the weakness of the member states' commitment to enlargement, and secondly in the additional hurdles it has raised for the enlargement process. At the very least, the IGC was expected to introduce more qualified majority voting (QMV) in a number of areas, to come to some agreement on limiting the number of Commissioners, to agree a reweighting of votes towards the larger member states, and to limit the future size of the European Parliament. In the event, apart from agreement on a limit on seats in the Parliament, this did not happen. The extension of QMV was very limited, even though the Commission had warned that the wider extension originally expected was inadequate; surprisingly, and significantly, it was Germany, under domestic pressures including from the *Länder*, that played an important role in limiting QMV.

Amid this general lack of progress, member states did agree a protocol to the Amsterdam Treaty stating that, at the time of the first accessions, there would be only one Commissioner per member state, as long as there had been an agreement on the reweighting of votes or a double majority voting system to compensate the larger member states. Consequently, before the first enlargement, the member states will have to find a way to agree if there is to be any institutional change before enlargement. Some member states – notably Belgium, France and Italy – have already made it clear that they will not support enlargement without further institutional reform as a prerequisite (*Financial Times,* 16 September 1997). Institutional reform, as much as policy reform, could thus be a serious hurdle for enlargement and could easily be used by reluctant member states as a means of delaying enlargement. The Commission calls for the reweighting decision to be taken well before 2000, but overall – presumably owing to its proximity to the IGC – Agenda 2000 says very little about institutional questions.

The protocol to the Amsterdam Treaty also states that there should be a comprehensive institutional review (another IGC) one year before the number of EU member states exceeds 20. This might suggest that another IGC will be necessary before the first enlargement, if the five CEE front-runners and Cyprus joined as a group, but as it is unlikely that all six will join together, it actually implies another blockage in the process for the other candidates. If some of the CEE applicants join the EU before there is another attempt to reform the institutions, then up to 20 EU member states will have to reach an agreement.

Flexibility in an enlarged EU
The difficulties of agreeing institutional reform – and the increasing difficulties as membership expands – have partly underlain the introduction of a flexibility clause in the Amsterdam Treaty. EMU and enlargement have been the two most important factors driving discussion of flexibility in recent years; however, flexibility is also seen as a way of dealing with political and economic diversity between member states, especially

where 'awkward' member states such as Britain have been seen as a brake on further integration. All of these factors lie behind recent discussion in academic and policy circles of concepts of differentiated integration, hard-core Europe, a multi-tier EU and flexibility (see Schäuble and Lamers 1994, Wallace and Wallace 1995, CEPR 1995, Weidenfeld and Janning 1996, Deubner 1995, Ehlermann 1995, Reflection Group 1995, CEC 1996).

The strongest pressure to include a flexibility clause or clauses in the Treaty at the IGC came from France and Germany. They issued a joint statement in autumn 1996 calling for flexibility to be used where decisions are currently taken by unanimity and for no member to have a veto over a decision to move ahead with only some member states. The actual flexibility clauses agreed at Amsterdam were weaker than this, reflecting member states' many concerns about the feasibility of flexibility and the dangers it might pose to the EU and its institutions. This tension recurs in discussions of flexibility: it could provide the key to future successful development of the EU, but it could lead to a splintering of the EU if wrongly developed.

Flexibility in the Treaty is very tightly circumscribed: it must involve a majority of member states and must not affect the rights and obligations of those member states that do not participate. The flexibility clause for the first pillar is more restricted still, stating that flexibility must not affect existing Community policies or programmes, impede trade and competition, affect the exclusive competences of the Community, or result in discrimination between member state nationals. Furthermore, although QMV can be used to decide to allow a flexible approach, any member state can veto it citing important, stated reasons of national interest. Although this flexibility clause may in retrospect be seen as an important first step, it does not look likely to provide the principal answer to the challenges of enlargement.

Despite the difficulties in developing forms of flexible integration, enlargement seems to demand some form of flexibility for two reasons. First, the combination of increased numbers and increased diversity in political, economic and security interests and approaches means not only that decision-making might seize up, but that operating procedures might also become highly inefficient (owing to increased numbers of people in meetings, more languages, an increase in possible coalitions and so on). Increased QMV cannot on its own solve these problems; it will also strain consensual decision-making processes, especially if individual member states are frequently in a minority or are outvoted on key developments.

Secondly, while the fact that this enlargement involves countries that are undergoing major economic transition and are lagging behind the current EU member states might seem simply to require the standard approach of applying transitional periods and derogations (leading to a multi-speed EU), in fact the size of the gap between the applicants and current members may mean that such a multi-speed EU would exist for a long time. Very long transitional periods could create tensions that threaten the unity of the Single Market; as is discussed in Chapter 5, negotiations are likely to lead to transitional periods, if not derogations, on the Structural Funds, CAP, free movement of people, aspects of environmental policy and other areas. These pressures, combined with the introduction of the single currency, make the development of some form of multi-tier EU look inevitable.

Enlargement may thus both demand and contribute to the development of a multi-tier EU; as yet it is unclear how this would be structured or function, and whether it would be sufficiently cohesive. There are three broad outcomes that can be envisaged if enlargement goes ahead. First, an enlarged EU could essentially reach a point of stasis, with adequate functioning of well-established areas, but lacking any further policy development and failing in particular to develop in problematic or newer policy areas (notably the common foreign and security policy, and justice and home affairs). Secondly, the EU could move towards defining a narrower core *acquis* while allowing flexibility in other areas; this outcome might be effective as long as the core *acquis* was sufficiently cohesive. Thirdly, the EU might enlarge on the basis of the current *acquis* with a core group of countries moving ahead in a number of areas; without effective institutional change, however, there would then be problems in operating the *acquis* and pressures might also build for the core group to splinter off from the rest.

In the absence of a genuine strategic overview of how to structure the future EU, one of these outcomes might emerge not through direct choice but by default, at the end of a sequence of step-by-step decisions on institutional reform and accession conditions; the resulting Union might be not so much a multi-tier as a patchwork EU.

Conclusion

The accession of 11 relatively poor countries, even in a series of smaller accessions with long transitional periods, will inevitably affect both Community finances and the way the Union works, although not necessarily all at once. The fact that enlargement might be spread over a period of ten to twenty years or more, starting at the earliest in 2002, means that reforms on the EU side are likely to occur in stages rather than in one great step. The Commission's proposals are sufficient to get the enlargement process going, but they are not enough to complete the reforms within the next financial perspective. The EU will have to return to the question of budgetary reform at least once (in 2006), and the whole process will take over a decade to complete. A major concern about this gradual process of adjustment is whether a proper strategic assessment of desirable changes will be made, and whether the outcomes for institutions and policies will be coherent and effective.

The potential for the enlargement process to be seriously disrupted by disagreements between member states over budgetary, policy and institutional reform is still high. Disagreements between member states over the budget could result in a protracted period of intra-EU negotiations, particularly over CAP reform, at the same time as enlargement negotiations are getting under way. Moreover, the fact that the Commission's budget proposals were presented in Agenda 2000 along with its enlargement proposals could increase the tendency for the two issues to be linked. If the budgetary disputes are bitter, this could reduce the appetite for enlargement still further in some member states, and it will certainly lessen generosity in allocating funds for the applicants in this financial perspective; once some of the CEE applicants become new members, the politics of the subsequent budget will become even more complicated.

The CEE applicants are highly unlikely to receive transfers on anything like the scale of those currently received by the Mediterranean members and Ireland, although there could be a substantial increase in comparison with current levels of assistance. Reforms are likely to reduce transfers to current recipients only gradually, and the CEE applicants will see only a very slow increase in the funds they receive, despite their very different stage of economic development. Moreover, the gap between the funds proposed for the countries expected to join first and those for the lagging countries threatens to widen the differences in their economic performance rather than to encourage catch-up; furthermore, given the political importance of EU funds, this allocation will fail to reassure the second-wave countries of the EU's commitment to them. Overall, a thousandth of EU GDP seems a very small price to pay for reuniting Europe and responding to post-1989 challenges. Even this allocation will be controversial, yet the conclusion has to be that the EU is attempting to achieve a historic step with remarkably low expenditure.

Member states are also attempting to take this step without having agreed what kind of institutional structure the enlarged EU should have. The failure of the IGC to agree even the initial institutional reforms needed for enlargement throws up additional hurdles for the process; there have been calls for further reforms to be a prerequisite for enlargement, suggesting that accessions could be blocked by reluctant member states on institutional grounds. The prospect of more members and more diversity makes the introduction of greater flexibility into the EU look inevitable; the danger is that, given the lack of a strategic overview for enlargement, an enlarged EU might not be able to function effectively if flexibility emerges as a result of piecemeal reforms.

Chapter 8

Security and external relations

Introduction

One of the most significant ways in which eastward expansion will be fundamentally different from previous enlargements of the EU is through its security dimension. A frequently cited aim of enlargement is to ensure stability and security in Europe by reuniting eastern Europe with the West. Yet beyond such statements lie a host of questions about the nature of security and how to achieve it. Two questions in particular stand out: does reuniting Europe require the CEE countries to be full members of all west European organizations and alliances? And what are the roles of these organizations and alliances now that the obvious and direct threats of the Cold War are gone? A full assessment of these questions is beyond the scope of this chapter, but they shape the debate about both the EU and NATO enlargements.

The implications of enlargement for the external relations of both the EU and CEE applicants are bound up in a wider framework of institutional change and security considerations. Because the Union's Common Foreign and Security Policy (CFSP) remains so limited, most of the serious discussion of defence and security matters among EU members takes place within the context of NATO, despite the different but overlapping memberships of the two organizations. Consequently, much of the discussion of the post-1989 security environment in both the EU and CEE concerns the future of NATO and its process of enlargement, which is determining the security aspects of EU enlargement in advance. NATO will enlarge first and take in only three CEE countries (at least initially), leaving the EU with a complex inheritance of security arrangements

109

among the CEE candidates. Looking beyond security, eastward enlargement could add new dimensions to EU external policy more generally, but probably only in the longer term.

The interface between the EU and NATO enlargements

Joining NATO has come to be seen by the CEE countries as the only credible guarantee of long-term defence. Initially, there seemed to be the possibility of alternatives to expanding the Western Alliance, and other, looser forms of defence cooperation with the West were proffered and accepted. Uncertainty over the development of European security after the end of the Cold War has resulted in a shifting pattern of security-related organizations, but, as the outlines of new European security priorities emerge, it has become increasingly clear that NATO remains the most credible security and defence body in Europe.

NATO itself faces the parallel challenges of reform and enlargement. After a long delay there has been progress since 1996 on both issues (Cornish 1997). The Berlin meeting of the North Atlantic Council in June 1996 established the underpinnings of NATO's 'internal adaptation' to new circumstances. (See *Agence Europe* 5/7/96, Atlantic Document No. 97.) A key element of reform is the development of a European Security and Defence Identity within rather than outside NATO, primarily through the creation of Combined Joint Task Force headquarters to plan and command operations, which could be led by the Western European Union (WEU), using NATO assets. Much in this concept has yet to be defined and there are still sharp differences between NATO members (notably France and the United States) in their ambitions for it. But despite the many uncertainties involved in the development of this European identity (see Cornish 1996), NATO has clearly emerged as the locus of policy-making in European security.

It is thus unsurprising that NATO membership has become the primary goal of the CEE countries' security and defence policies. They have proved willing to participate in a range of security-building and defence-related activities in cooperation with Western security organizations, but most CEE policy-makers remain adamant that these must be complementary to full NATO membership or part of a strategy of progress towards it. However, NATO's decision to offer membership to only three applicants (Poland, Hungary and the Czech Republic) at Madrid in July 1997, and the political debates surrounding it, have forced reconsideration of prospects for the others to join. NATO has stated that the alliance remains open to further members and at Madrid made special reference to the candidacies of Romania and Slovenia. Nevertheless, if ratification of NATO expansion proves painful and prolonged, particularly in the United States, the process of taking in further new members could slow down or even stall. This possibility, with the certainty that the other applicants will not join NATO this century, has increased interest in EU enlargement.

The CEE countries' concerns about the security aspects of EU membership are closely linked to their prospects for NATO membership. The small number of countries that join NATO in the first wave will take on a similar range of defence interests to those of current EU members, whereas those that join the EU but not NATO are likely to be keener to bolster the security aspects of EU membership, including the implicit security framework it offers. NATO enlargement is also a crucial factor in the EU's discussions of the security and defence aspects of its own enlargement because of NATO's key role and the timing of the two enlargements. The small scale of the NATO expansion planned for 1999 has thus changed the environment for EU enlargement, first by differentiating overtly between the applicants for EU membership, and secondly by influencing the outlook for EU foreign policy, security and defence arrangements.

Members and timing

NATO and EU members frequently refer to the two enlargements as 'parallel processes' in order to dampen expectations that one will affect the timing and contents of the other. This formula is tenable in so far as different criteria apply for membership of the two structures; nevertheless, NATO's expansion influences views of the progress of different CEE countries towards Western norms not just in terms of their military capabilities and security policies. NATO has laid down a wide range of political as well as military criteria (see NATO 1995), and acceptance by the organization sets an important seal of approval on the first entrants' progress in political transition. Although NATO and the EU have different entry criteria, the lack of discussion and coordination between the two bodies over their respective enlargements should be remedied.

The matrix in Figure 8.1 shows the prospects of the ten CEE countries for joining NATO and the EU. The enlargements may not proceed in waves, but countries' prospects are currently grouped fairly clearly for EU membership; however, it is important to note that the second and third groups for NATO membership are more fluid. The current outlook

111

Figure 8.1: Matrix of applicants' prospects for EU and NATO membership

		NATO		
		1st group	2nd group	3rd group
EU	1st group	Czech Republic Hungary Poland	Slovenia	Estonia
	2nd group		Slovakia	Latvia Lithuania
	3rd group		Romania	Bulgaria

is for a small initial NATO expansion, and probably a fairly small EU enlargement to begin with, but the EU may end up widening more than NATO does.

Given that the first new NATO members are also among the leading contenders for the first wave of EU enlargement, the two processes will be mutually reinforcing in bringing the Czech Republic, Hungary and Poland into European structures ahead of the others, although not all those in the first round of negotiations will necessarily join the EU at the same time. These three countries are on the swiftest and strongest track in terms of integration into all Western institutions. Slovenia and Estonia are both in the first wave of EU negotiations, but, whereas Slovenia was considered for NATO membership and is likely to be part of any next wave of NATO expansion, Estonia's prospects of joining the Alliance are more remote.

The remaining five countries comprise the 'double outs' (in the highlighted box in the matrix), which are not likely to join either organization quickly. The extent to which these countries' prospects for joining NATO and the EU begin to establish new dividing lines in Europe, with worrying implications for stability, depends partly on the relationships and reassurance that the two organizations offer them. They do not form an undifferentiated group, however. Slovakia is seen as not too far behind for EU membership, given its economic strengths, but the doubts about its democratic credentials are an obstacle to its joining either organization. Latvia and Lithuania are behind Estonia in the queue for EU membership, primarily because of economic problems, and they could start negotiations fairly quickly after the front-runners; however, they share with Estonia a relatively unfavourable position with regard to NATO enlargement because of Russian opposition to their candidacies and perceptions of indefensibility among some NATO members.

By contrast, Romania had high hopes of joining NATO and is in a good position if and when there is a second expansion of the Alliance, but it is clearly far from joining the EU given its economic conditions. Bulgaria is in the most excluded position, being far behind in economic terms and also a long way from NATO membership. Unless NATO expands further, current prospects for EU membership suggest that a new dividing line could develop, not between the five in the EU first wave and the rest, but cutting off southeastern Europe; both EU and NATO policies should focus on avoiding this danger.

A critical question for ensuring a stable and secure future for all the post-communist countries and for the West is how members of the Western Alliance should deal with the CEE countries left outside both the EU and NATO – in some cases for several years. Failing to achieve the central foreign policy goal of integration could have an impact on these countries' domestic politics (see Chapter 5) and on bilateral relations with their neighbours.

Membership aspirations have already acted as a catalyst in improving bilateral relations in CEE and with countries further east. The EU and NATO have so far pursued a strategy of insisting that any regional disputes must be fully resolved before CEE countries can join. Aspirations to join Western organizations have undoubtedly been an important factor in forcing several CEE countries into formal settlements of minority and border issues such as basic treaties (see Wohlfeld 1997).

Nevertheless, although conditionality has had such effects, more may be needed to prevent the cold reality of differentiation among applicants from dividing their foreign policy interests, especially if processes of enlargement are prolonged. Although CEE countries may seem to have little alternative to Western orientation, a very protracted process of accessions could nevertheless provoke greater domestic debate about whether to pursue a more independent foreign policy, and it could fuel nationalism. So far the EU's approach has been almost exclusively bilateral, with sub-regional initiatives to encourage cooperation and integration between the CEE countries coming primarily from individual member states. But if the process of enlargement stretches over 15 years or more, it will become increasingly important for the EU to develop initiatives to facilitate economic integration and political cooperation among the applicants.

As countries join at different times, the EU's borders will divide CEE. There could be tensions over borders between applicants, as arrangements such as the Czech–Slovak customs union and visa-free access to Hungary are disrupted. The various initiatives aimed at Baltic integration could also be weakened. These concerns over the effect on bilateral relations are shared by the front-runner countries, and there is considerable emphasis from them on the need to support reforms in the other five countries. It is understandable that Estonia would support the other Baltic states, Poland would support Lithuania, the Czech Republic would try to help Slovakia, and Hungary would be concerned about Slovakia and Romania. In this respect, it was very important that the Commission recommended opening negotiations with more than just the three countries invited to join NATO. The inclusion of a Baltic country was particularly important in sending a signal to the applicants and to Russia that this would not be just a central European enlargement.

There is also the danger that non-applicants left outside the EU and NATO, such as Russia and Ukraine will feel threatened by the enlarged organizations on their doorsteps if their own prospects for joining are remote. From this perspective, it will be extremely important for the EU to develop interim arrangements to ensure continuing political and economic cooperation between the enlarged Union and the countries on its new eastern and southern borders. EU enlargement will not fulfil its stated purpose if, in shifting its borders eastwards, it fails to ensure stability on its new peripheries. The question of relations with non-applicants is especially important where there are extensive economic linkages or populations of mixed ethnic origins: what impact will accession have on relations between Slovenia and Croatia, Bulgaria and the former Yugoslavia, Ukraine and its western frontier, Romania and Moldova?

Until recently, there seems to have been little opposition in Moscow to any country in CEE joining the EU, with attention focused almost exclusively on the NATO question. However, it is possible that the security aspects of EU enlargement could become more of an issue in Russian foreign policy, and there have already been some tensions in trade relations with the EU. Prime Minister Victor Chernomyrdin rapidly announced Russia's interest in eventually joining the EU after Agenda 2000 was published (*Financial Times*, 19/20 July 1997): this move may have more to do with raising Russia's international profile and reminding the EU of its interest in the CEE applicants than with any serious ambition to intensify relations beyond the partnership and cooperation agreement signed in 1994. Russia is also moving deliberately slowly in signing border treaties with Estonia and Latvia, which are essential if they are to be eligible to join the EU and NATO; a treaty on Lithuania's border with Kaliningrad was finally signed in October 1997 and is awaiting ratification.

Foreign and security policy-making in an enlarged EU

The EU had very little in the way of formal foreign policy and security mechanisms before Maastricht, when the Common Foreign and Security Policy was established as the 'second pillar' of the Union. As it has developed since, CFSP is not a policy, or even a set of policies, but rather a consultation mechanism between governments within an EU institutional framework. Under the Amsterdam Treaty, CFSP is to include 'all questions related to the security of the Union, including the progressive framing of a common defence policy ... which might in time lead to a common defence, should the European Council so decide' (Article J.7). EU members have been too divided to move far towards a common defence policy, and the process of reforming NATO has muted traditional demands from some member states for a self-contained European security and defence identity, at least for the time being.

There are two main problems encountered in CFSP, and both are likely to be exacerbated by enlargement. The first is the diversity of member states' foreign policy preferences. Even if they all recognize the same fundamental security and defence interests, individual states accord different priorities to developments, both within and outside Europe, and have different foreign policy approaches to them, including varying degrees of willingness to involve themselves in conflicts. In addition, four EU members are neutral countries. The different nuances in policy towards the Middle East and Bosnia in particular have resulted in a string of failures to agree on measures for a common foreign policy which has helped to denigrate the whole idea of a CFSP in the eyes of the public and media. This problem will be increased by enlargement as new member states bring in diverse perspectives on foreign policy issues ranging from relations with the rest of the former communist bloc to interests in the Middle East.

The second problem is the institutional framework for CFSP. Since Maastricht, the current 15 members have experienced difficulty in achieving unanimity even on issues where member states' positions are not far apart, and there are concerns that the addition of further members will increase the number of potential vetoes for any decision. There has

115

been a very wide range of views across member states on how CFSP could and should be improved, and an equal diversity of opinions on how it should be adapted to fit a much larger and more heterogeneous EU. This lack of consensus, combined with the absence of immediate pressure to improve effectiveness and the speed of decision-making, resulted in only relatively minor changes to the CFSP framework in the Amsterdam Treaty. A flexibility arrangement was introduced by instituting a new instrument, the 'common strategy', and a form of constructive abstention, but their potential interpretation was left ambiguous.

The institutional changes in the Treaty may prove insufficient to improve the effectiveness of CFSP to member states' satisfaction, particularly after enlargement. If perceptions of immobility and lack of credibility increase, ambitious member states will have a strong incentive to form groups to pursue particular policy goals; thus, even if use of the new flexibility arrangements is limited, *de facto* flexibility could emerge in the form of groups of member states pursuing foreign policy goals not shared by the others, as has already happened in cases such as Operation Alba for Albania.

Enlargement has the potential to reduce the scope for CFSP to develop into a more substantive policy and for the EU to move towards a common defence. It will increase the divergence between member states' foreign policy interests, making it even more difficult to form coherent joint policies, and these problems could drive the EU further towards introducing formal flexibility into the second pillar to get around them. The danger is that flexibility could weaken the formation of a common policy and reduce the global weight of EU external positions because these would not be shared by all member states. Flexibility will be necessary to allow an enlarged EU to function, and it has the potential to work; but the question remains whether it will cause fragmentation of positions and make the EU look ineffective as an external actor.

The role of the WEU

The Western European Union's future role in European foreign and security policy is unclear. The IGC did not resolve debates between member states about its future relationship with the EU, most importantly whether it should be merged with the EU, possibly in the form of a 'fourth pillar', or remain semi-autonomous. The WEU's role as a political bridge between the EU and NATO may increase in importance after enlargement, especially if not all members of an enlarged EU are members of

NATO, although it still remains essentially a 'virtual' organization. Under the Berlin compromise, the WEU seems likely to end up as a subset of NATO members, carrying out humanitarian and peace-keeping missions (the Petersberg tasks) using NATO assets when the United States and Canada do not want to take part. In this respect, the WEU could become the main coordinating body for carrying out CFSP joint actions with defence implications now that the Petersberg tasks are to be brought into the Treaty on European Union.

The WEU's role will thus be changing in parallel with the process of EU enlargement. This complicates the process of defining the CEE candidates' relationship with the WEU. The CEE-10 are currently 'associate partners' of the WEU, and they would have to join NATO to be eligible for full WEU membership. The WEU's different forms of membership (full members, associates, observers and associate partners) have served as a way of bringing neutral EU members into the security policy-making process without requiring them to join the Western Alliance, and the Amsterdam Treaty continues this arrangement. This situation would clearly have to be changed if the EU and WEU were to merge, and the role of the CEE applicants would depend on the solution found for the neutral EU members. It is possible that some of the currently neutral members of the EU might change their stances and join both NATO and the WEU while the process of EU enlargement is going on; such an outcome would have the potential to alter the EU's perspective on its role in security and defence in the longer term.

Conclusion

The parallel processes of EU and NATO enlargement run the risk of reinforcing the division between those countries in CEE that are already most stable and secure and those that are not included. Yet there is little coordination between the two bodies to ensure that the applicants with more remote prospects for joining one or both organizations are not alienated by the processes of enlargement.

It is thus extremely important that EU enlargement not only includes a wider range of applicants than NATO but also is accompanied by measures to ensure long-term political and economic cooperation with the wider Europe. The start of EU negotiations with Estonia and Slovenia as well as the Czech Republic, Hungary and Poland is very significant in widening the geo-political scope of the process and in opening up Baltic and southeastern European dimensions to it. But it is also important to look beyond these front-runner applicants; a renewed commitment to eventual membership and a comprehensive strategy for progressively involving the five countries outside negotiations in EU processes is needed for the period before they are realistically likely to join. This would do much to reassure and support those countries that might not join for many years, helping to ensure their stability and sending a signal both to their own populations and to other countries that the EU is concerned about and willing to facilitate their process of reintegration into the international community.

The EU also needs to develop initiatives to foster intraregional cooperation and integration, particularly in terms of economic interpenetration between applicants and with the rest of the region. Greater attention to this would also lessen the risk of the enlarged EU and NATO being seen as a fortress that threatens those countries remaining far from the prospect of membership.

Chapter 9

Conclusions

This book has analysed the political, economic and security issues involved in enlarging the EU eastwards up to the point at which negotiations are about to start. Launching the single currency continues to attract prime political attention and commitment in the EU, but the two biggest and most complex challenges facing the EU are enlargement and unemployment. Whereas the current consensus is that tackling unemployment is a task primarily for each individual member state, enlargement requires support, commitment and leadership from the EU as a whole. The end of the Cold War means that the EU's overarching aims of promoting peace and prosperity now apply across Europe and not just in the West; after all, the EU's founding treaty states that membership is open to all European countries. The war in the former Yugoslavia was the most critical European challenge of the post-Cold War period, and the EU's failure to deal effectively with it seriously undermines its claims to be responding strategically to the post-1989 environment. If the EU is to remain relevant in the 21st century, it cannot afford to fail in enlarging eastwards and responding effectively to the needs of CEE countries in transition, and these countries stretch beyond the current applicants.

The enlargement process involving the current applicants is now under way, and negotiations will start with the five front-runners in the first half of 1998. The process has been slow and this lack of speed looks likely to continue. There is no overarching strategy for constructing a European Union of 26 or more member states. Rather, the Commission provides in Agenda 2000 the outlines of a strategy for getting to the start of negotiations and for enabling the EU to cope with the first few accessions in terms of their impact on the EU's policies and institutions. The EU has typically developed in this way – step-by-step and frequently technocratically – and politicians' time-horizons are short. But the lack of an overall strategy means that the process is likely to unfold in an uneven way that may be damaging rather than beneficial both to the applicants and to the future of the EU and its current members.

The enlargement process is suffering from a lack of leadership as well as strategy. Motivations for enlargement vary across the member states, and some countries' commitment is very weak. There is a range of concerns among member states about enlargement; these are not primarily about the impact of economic integration through trade and investment, since this integration is already occurring in advance of accession, but more about the institutional functioning of the EU and the impact of enlargement on future integration, and about budgetary costs, particularly the impact on existing transfers and policies. There are also fears about the impact of enlargement on sensitive sectors (especially agriculture) and about allowing free movement of labour.

This set of concerns provides the background against which negotiations will start in 1998 with the Czech Republic, Estonia, Hungary, Poland, Slovenia and Cyprus. The EU's *avis* on the ten CEE applicants have not been highly controversial; but there has been disagreement among member states about whether to start negotiations with all ten applicants or only with the front-runners. The decision to start with just five CEE applicants raises the question of how to develop closer relations with the remaining five. Agenda 2000 proposes the establishment of Accession Partnership agreements with all the applicants to review progress towards taking on the EU's *acquis*, and also proposes holding a regular European Conference for all applicants, probably including Turkey. However, the European Commission's budget proposals, if agreed, would give the front-runners more than twice the amount allocated to the second group of applicants. Combined with the questionable commitment of member states to enlarging to all ten CEE applicants, this strategy pays inadequate attention to the lagging group.

The EU needs to reaffirm its commitment to their eventual membership and should ensure greater equality of financial treatment. Other specific measures should be adopted to reassure the lagging group that they will not be excluded: greater opening of agricultural markets would be one helpful step, and removing the visa requirements faced by Bulgarians and Romanians would be another. As the strategy stands, the EU is paying insufficient attention to the impact of its decisions on the political environment and reform processes in the second group. This group also constitutes the 'double outs' that are not included in NATO's first wave of new members either. There has been a serious lack of coordination and even communication between NATO and the EU on the joint impact of their respective enlargement decisions, and this should be remedied.

The EU's commitment to enlargement would also be clearer for all applicants if the process moved more swiftly. The EU cannot guarantee a specific accession date, but it could set a desired time-frame for the initial accessions and subsequent ones. Not only would this provide a clearer signal of commitment to the applicants, it would also provide a framework for beginning to develop a proper enlargement strategy. As it stands, negotiations could be lengthy both because of the applicants' distance from meeting the conditions, and also because of the necessary policy and institutional reforms in the EU. The negotiators will have to decide how much of the *acquis* the applicants must take on before they join and how much subsequently through the use of transition periods. Many difficult decisions loom, and negotiations could be further complicated by the proposed Accession Partnership agreements, which overlap with negotiations and could conflict with them. On current trends the first accessions are likely to occur nearer 2005 than 2002; adopting a time-frame for the process could help to bring them closer to 2002. The perspective for the lagging applicants is unclear; some might join within two or three years of the front-runners (or even overtake them in negotiations) but others could take until 2010 or later. By this stage, other European countries are likely to have applied to join; enlarging the EU could thus continue over the next twenty years.

With regard to institutional issues, the Amsterdam Treaty failed to take even the small initial steps necessary for enlargement. Institutional issues could delay or even block enlargement, and they may be addressed *ad hoc* as new members join in small groups. It seems likely that the EU will evolve into some form of multi-tier institution as it enlarges; it will thus be a rather different organization from the current one, and there is a danger that it could become very weak or could even splinter. The EU needs to give more strategic consideration now to what a Union of 26 or more member states would be like.

Ensuring that the EU enlarges eastwards successfully for all con-cerned is a difficult but crucial aim. It will require increased leadership and commitment, radical strategies, and adept bargaining skills to deal with the different interests and concerns of the countries involved. The enlargement process is on the road, but all these elements will be needed to ensure that it moves forward swiftly and successfully.

References

Chapter 2

Baldwin, Richard E. (1994), *Towards an Integrated Europe*. London: Centre for Economic Policy Research.

Baldwin, Richard E. (1995), 'The Eastern Enlargement of the European Union', *European Economic Review* 39, 474–81.

Baldwin, Richard E., Joseph F. François, and Richard Portes (1997), 'The Costs and Benefits of Eastern Enlargement', *Economic Policy* 24 (April).

Brown, Drusilla K., Alan V. Deardorff, Simeon D. Djankov, and Robert M. Stern (1997), 'An Economic Assessment of the Integration of Czechoslovakia, Hungary and Poland into the European Union', in *Europe's Economy Looks East: Implications for Germany and the European Union*, ed. Stanley W. Black. Cambridge: Cambridge University Press, 23–63.

Cadot, Olivier, Riccardo Faini, and Jaime de Melo (1995), 'Early Trade Patterns under the Europe Agreements: France, Germany and Italy', *European Economic Review* 39, 601–10.

CEPR (1990), *The Impact of Eastern Europe (Monitoring European Integration, 1)*. London: Centre for Economic Policy Research.

Collins, S. M. and D. Rodrik (1991), *Eastern Europe and the Soviet Union in the World Economy*. Washington DC: Institute for International Economics.

Commission of the European Communities (CEC) (1994), 'Trade Liberalization with Central and Eastern Europe', *European Economy*, Supplement A (No. 7), 1–20.

CEC (1997), *Towards Greater Economic Integration: The European Union's Financial Assistance, Trade Policy and Investments for Central and Eastern Europe*. Brussels: Directorate General IA.

References – Chapter 2

Dittus, Peter and Palle S. Andersen (1995), 'Sectoral and Employment Effects of the Opening Up of Eastern Europe', in *Western Europe in Transition: The Impact of the Opening Up of Eastern Europe and the Former Soviet Union*, eds. Patrick de Fontenay, Giorgio Gomel, and Eduard Hochreiter. Washington DC: International Monetary Fund, 55–90.

Drábek, Zdenek and Alasdair Smith (1995), *Trade Performance and Trade Policy in Central and Eastern Europe*. Discussion Paper No. 1182. London: Centre for Economic Policy Research.

EBRD (1997), *Transition Report*. London: European Bank for Reconstruction and Development.

Estrin, Saul (ed.) (1994), *Privatization in Central and Eastern Europe*. London: Longman.

Estrin, Saul, Kirsty Hughes, and Sarah Todd (1997), *Foreign Direct Investment in Central and Eastern Europe: Multinationals in Transition*. London: RIIA/Pinter.

Eurostat (various issues), *External and Intra-EU Trade: Monthly Statistics*. Luxembourg: Statistical Office of the European Communities.

Faini, Riccardo and Richard Portes (1995), 'Opportunities Outweigh Adjustment: The Political Economy of Trade with Central and Eastern Europe', in *European Union Trade with Eastern Europe: Adjustments and Opportunities*, eds. Riccardo Faini and Richard Portes. London: Centre for Economic Policy Research, 1–18.

Grabbe, Heather (1997), 'Trade and FDI in Central and Eastern Europe: The Roles of Germany and the United Kingdom Compared', mimeo.

Halpern, László (1995), 'Comparative Advantage and Likely Trade Pattern of the CEECs', in *European Union Trade with Eastern Europe: Adjustments and Opportunities*, eds. Riccardo Faini and Richard Portes. London: Centre for Economic Policy Research, 61–85.

Hamilton, Carl B. and L. Alan Winters (1992), 'Opening Up International Trade with Eastern Europe', *Economic Policy* 14 (April), 77–116.

Hughes, Gordon and Paul Hare (1992), 'Trade Policy and Restructuring in Eastern Europe', in *Trade, Payments and Adjustment in Central and Eastern Europe*, eds. John Flemming and J. M. C. Rollo. London: Royal Institute of International Affairs, 181–210.

Hughes, Kirsty (1996), 'European Enlargement, Competitiveness and Integration', in *Competitiveness, Subsidiarity and Industrial Policy*, eds. Pat Devine, Yannis Katsoulacos, and Roger Sugden. London and New York: Routledge.

IMF (various issues), *Direction of Trade Statistics Yearbook*. Washington DC: International Monetary Fund.

Inotai, András (1994), 'Central and Eastern Europe', in *Reviving the European Union*, eds. Randall C. Henning, E. Hochreiter, and G. Hufbauer. Washington DC: Institute for International Economics, 139–76.

Messerlin, Patrick A. (1992), 'The Association Agreements between the EC and Central Europe: Trade Liberalization vs Constitutional Failure?', in *Trade, Payments and Adjustment in Central and Eastern Europe*, eds. John Flemming and J. M. C. Rollo. London: Royal Institute of International Affairs, 111–43.

Neven, Damien (1995), 'Trade Liberalization with Eastern Nations: How Sensitive?', in *European Union Trade with Eastern Europe: Adjustments and Opportunities*, eds. Riccardo Faini and Richard Portes. London: Centre for Economic Policy Research, 19–60.

Nuti, D. Mario (1997), 'European Community Response to the Transition: Aid, Trade Access and Enlargement', in *EU–CEECs Integration: Policies and Markets at Work*, eds. Salvatore Baldone and Fabio Sdogati. Milan: Franco Angeli, 3–14.

Rollo, Jim and Alasdair Smith (1993), 'The Political Economy of Eastern European Trade with the European Community: Why So Sensitive?', *Economic Policy* 16 (April), 139–181.

Takla, Lina (1996), 'Competitiveness: An Analysis of Czech, Polish and Hungarian Trade Patterns', mimeo, June.

UN (1997), *World Investment Report*. New York and Geneva: United Nations.

Vittas, Hari and Polo Mauro (1997), 'Potential Trade with Core and Periphery: Industry Differences in Trade Patterns', in *Europe's Economy Looks East: Implications for Germany and the European Union*, ed. Stanley W. Black. Cambridge: Cambridge University Press, 67–96.

Wang, Z. and L. A. Winters (1991), *The Trading Potential of Eastern Europe*. Discussion Paper No. 610. London: Centre for Economic Policy Research.

Winters, L. Alan, (ed.) (1995), *Foundations of an Open Economy: Trade Laws and Institutions for Eastern Europe*. London: Centre for Economic Policy Research.

World Bank (1996), *World Development Report 1996: From Plan to Market*. New York: Oxford University Press.

Wyplosz, Charles (1995), 'Trade and European Labour Markets', in *Western Europe in Transition: The Impact of the Opening Up of Eastern Europe and the Former Soviet Union*, eds. Patrick de Fontenay, Giorgio Gomel, and Eduard Hochreiter. Washington DC: International Monetary Fund, 55–90.

Chapter 3

Baldwin, Richard E. (1994), *Towards an Integrated Europe*. London: Centre for Economic Policy Research.

Commission of the European Communities (CEC) (1995), *Towards Greater Economic Integration: The European Union's Financial Assistance and Trade Policy for Central and Eastern Europe and the New Independent States*. Brussels: Directorate General IA.

Court of Auditors (1997), 'Report', reproduced in *Official Journal* No. C/175 and quoted in *Agence Europe* No. 7017, 16 July.

Drábek, Zdenek and Alasdair Smith (1995), *Trade Performance and Trade Policy in Central and Eastern Europe*. Discussion Paper No. 1182. London: Centre for Economic Policy Research.

EBRD (1994), *Transition Report*. London: European Bank for Reconstruction and Development.

EBRD (1995), *Transition Report*. London: European Bank for Reconstruction and Development.

EBRD (1997), *Transition Report*. London: European Bank for Reconstruction and Development.

European Council (1993), 'European Council in Copenhagen: Presidency Conclusions', 21–22 June.

Faini, Riccardo and Richard Portes (1995), 'Opportunities Outweigh Adjustment: The Political Economy of Trade with Central and Eastern Europe', in *European Union Trade with Eastern Europe: Adjustments and Opportunities*, eds. Riccardo Faini and Richard Portes. London: Centre for Economic Policy Research, 1–18.

Hamilton, Carl B. and L. Alan Winters (1992), 'Opening Up International Trade with Eastern Europe', *Economic Policy* 14 (April), 77–116.

Inotai, András (1994), 'Central and Eastern Europe', in *Reviving the European Union*, eds. Randall C. Henning, E. Hochreiter, and G. Hufbauer. Washington DC: Institute for International Economics, 139–76.

Inotai, András (1995), 'From Association Agreements to Full Membership? The Dynamics of Relations between the Central and Eastern European Countries and the European Union,' Institute for World Economics Working Paper No. 52, Budapest.

Messerlin, Patrick (1992), 'The Association Agreements between the EC and Central Europe: Trade Liberalization vs. Constitutional Failure?', in *Trade, Payments and Adjustment in Central and Eastern Europe*, eds. John Flemming and J. M. C. Rollo. London: Royal Institute of International Affairs, 111–43.

Messerlin, Patrick (1995), 'Central and East European Countries' Trade Laws in the Light of International Experience', in *Foundations of an Open*

Economy: Trade Laws and Institutions for Eastern Europe, ed. L. Alan Winters. London: Centre for Economic Policy Research, 40–63.

Nuti, D. Mario (1997), 'European Community Response to the Transition: Aid, Trade Access and Enlargement' in *EU–CEEs Integration: Policies and Markets at Work*, eds. Salvatore Baldone and Fabio Sdogati. Milan: FrancoAngeli, 3–14.

Preston, Christopher (1997), 'Poland and EU Membership: Current Issues and Future Prospects', Paper prepared for the UACES conference 'Enlarging the European Union', Birmingham, July.

Rollo, Jim and Alasdair Smith (1993), 'The Political Economy of Eastern European Trade with the European Community: Why So Sensitive?', *Economic Policy* 16 (April), 139–81.

Sapir, André, (1995), 'The Europe Agreements: Implications for Trade Laws and Institutions', in *Foundations of an Open Economy: Trade Laws and Institutions for Eastern Europe*, ed. L. Alan Winters. London: Centre for Economic Policy Research, 89–107.

Smith, Alasdair, Peter Holmes, Ulrich Sedelmeir, Edward Smith, Helen Wallace, and Alasdair Young (1996), *The European Union and Central and Eastern Europe: Pre-Accession Strategies*. Brighton: Sussex European Institute.

Winters, L. Alan (ed.) (1995a), *Foundations of an Open Economy: Trade Laws and Institutions for Eastern Europe*. London: Centre for Economic Policy Research.

Winters, L. Alan (1995b), 'Liberalization of the European Steel Trade', in *European Union Trade with Eastern Europe: Adjustments and Opportunities*, eds. Riccardo Faini and Richard Portes. London: Centre for Economic Policy Research, 201–235.

World Bank (1997), *Poland Country Economic Memorandum: Reform and Growth on the Road to the EU*. Report No. 16858-POL. Washington DC: World Bank.

Chapter 4

Batt, Judy (1996), *The New Slovakia: National Identity, Political Integration and the Return to Europe*. Discussion Paper No. 65. London: Royal Institute of International Affairs.

Commission of the European Communities (CEC) (1997), *Agenda 2000: For a Stronger and Wider Union*. Luxembourg: OOPEC.

Crawford, Beverly (1995), 'Post-Communist Political Economy: A Framework for the Analysis of Reform', in *Markets, States and Democracy: The Political Economy of Post-Communist Transformation*, ed. Beverly Crawford. Boulder, Colo.: Westview Press, 3–42.

Hausner, Jerzy, Bob Jessop, and Klaus Nielsen (1995), 'Institutional Change in
  Post-Socialism', in *Strategic Choice and Path-Dependency in Post-
  Socialism: Institutional Dynamics in the Transformation Process*, eds.
  Jerzy Hausner, Bob Jessop, and Klaus Nielsen. Aldershot, Hants: Edward
  Elgar, 3–46.
Kaldor, Mary and Ivan Vejvoda (1997), 'Democratization in Central and
  Eastern European Countries', *International Affairs* 73 (1), 59–82.
Linz, Juan J. and Alfred Stepan (1996), *Problems of Democratic Transition
  and Consolidation*, Baltimore: Johns Hopkins University Press.
Schöpflin, George (1996), 'Post-Communism and Nationalism in Central and
  Eastern Europe 1990–1996', Paper delivered at the ISA–JAIR Conference,
  19–21 September, Tokyo.
Smith, Alasdair, Peter Holmes, Ulrich Sedelmeir, Edward Smith, Helen
  Wallace, and Alasdair Young (1996), *The European Union and Central
  and Eastern Europe: Pre-Accession Strategies*. Brighton: Sussex European
  Institute.

Chapter 5

Avery, Graham (1994), 'The European Union's Enlargement Negotiations',
  Oxford International Review (Summer), 27–32.
Grabbe, Heather and Kirsty Hughes (1998), 'The Impact of Enlargement on
  EU Trade and Industrial Policy', in *Enlargements of the European Union:
  Past, Present and Future*, eds. J. Redmond and G. Rosenthal. Boulder,
  Colo.: Lynne Rienner.

Chapter 6

Bohatá, Marie and Jan Mládek (1997), 'The Political Economy of EU
  Enlargement: The Czech Republic', Draft paper for ACE Project P95-
  2106-R.
Eurobarometer (1997), *Central and Eastern Eurobarometer* No. 7. Brussels:
  Commission of the European Communities.
Milanovich, Natasha Pichler (1997), 'The Political Economy of EU
  Enlargement: Political Outlook, Debates and Public Opinion on EU
  Enlargement in Slovenia', Draft paper for ACE Project P95-2106-R.
Rose, Richard and Christian Haerpfer (1995), 'Democracy and Enlarging the
  European Union Eastwards', *Journal of Common Market Studies* 33,
  427–50.
Shikova, Ingrid and Krassimir Nikolov (1997), 'The Political Economy of the
  Eastern Enlargement of the European Union: A Case Study on Bulgaria',
  Draft paper for ACE Project P95-2106-R.

Tamási, Péter (1997), 'Political Outlook, Debate and Public Opinion on Enlargement: the Hungarian Case Study', Draft paper for ACE Project P95-2106-R.

Chapter 7
Anderson, K. and R. Tyers (1993), *Implications of EC Expansion for European Agricultural Policies, Trade and Welfare*. CEPR Discussion Paper No. 829. London: Centre for Economic Policy Research.

Baldwin, Richard E. (1994), *Towards an Integrated Europe*. London: Centre for Economic Policy Research.

Brenton, Paul and Daniel Gros (1993), 'The Budgetary Implications of EC Enlargement', Centre for European Policy Studies Working Document No. 78, Brussels.

CEPR (1995), *Flexible Integration: Towards a More Effective and Democratic Europe* (*Monitoring European Integration*, 6). London: Centre for Economic Policy Research.

Commission of the European Communities (CEC) (1993), 'Stable Money – Sound Finances: Community Public Finance in the Perspective of EMU', *European Economy* 53.

CEC (1995), *Study on Alternative Strategies for the Development of Relations in the Field of Agriculture between the EU and the Associated Countries with a View to Future Accession of these Countries*. CSE(95) 607. Brussels: OOPEC.

CEC (1996), *First Cohesion Report*. COM(96) 542 final. Brussels: OOPEC.

CEC (1997), *Agenda 2000: For a Stronger and Wider Union*. Luxembourg: OOPEC.

Deubner, Christian (1995), *Deutsche Europapolitik: Von Maastricht nach Kerneuropa?* Baden-Baden: Nomos.

EBRD (1995), *Transition Report*. London: European Bank for Reconstruction and Development.

Ehlermann, Claus-Dieter (1995), *Increased Differentiation or Stronger Uniformity*. EUI Working Paper RSC No. 95/21. Florence: European University Institute.

Hartmann, Monika (1996), 'Implications of EU East Enlargement for the CAP', Paper presented at the CREDIT conference 'CAP Reform: What Next?', Nottingham University, 26 March.

House of Lords, Select Committee on the European Communities (1996), *Enlargement and Common Agricultural Policy Reform*, HL Paper 92. London: HMSO.

Inotai, András (1994), 'The System of Criteria for Hungary's Accession to the

European Union', Institute for World Economics Trends in World Economy No. 76, Budapest.

Reflection Group (1995), 'Reflection Group's Report to the Intergovernmental Conference' (Westendorp Report), Brussels, 5 December.

Schäuble, Wolfgang and Karl Lamers (1994), *Reflections on European Policy*. Bonn: CDU/CSU–Fraktion des Deutschen Bundestags.

Tangermann, Stefan (1996), 'An Ex-Post Review of the 1992 MacSharry Reform', Paper presented at the CREDIT conference 'CAP Reform: What Next?', Nottingham University, 26 March.

Wallace, Helen (1996), 'Fitting the European Union for Europe', in *Perspectives on Europe*, ed. European Policy Forum. London: European Policy Forum, 4–18.

Wallace, Helen and William Wallace (1995), 'Flying Together in a Larger and More Diverse European Union', Working Document, Study for the Netherlands Scientific Council for Government Policy, June.

Weidenfeld, Werner and Josef Janning (1996), 'The New Europe: Strategies for Differentiated Integration', Paper presented at the International Bertelsmann Forum, Petersberg, 19–20 January.

World Bank (1996), *World Development Report 1996: From Plan to Market*. New York: Oxford University Press.

Chapter 8

Cornish, Paul (1996), 'European Security: The End of Architecture and the New NATO', *International Affairs* 72 (4), 751–769.

Cornish, Paul (1997), *Partnership in Crisis: The US, Europe and the Fall and Rise of NATO*. Chatham House Paper. London: RIIA/Pinter.

NATO (1995), 'Study on NATO Enlargement', Internal study presented to Cooperation Partners, 28 September.

Wohlfeld, Monika, ed. (1997), *The Effects of Enlargement on Bilateral Relations in Central and Eastern Europe*. Chaillot Paper 26. Paris: Institute for Security Studies, Western European Union.

Chatham House
Papers

 THE ROYAL INSTITUTE OF
INTERNATIONAL AFFAIRS

Partnership in Crisis
The US, Europe and the Fall and Rise of NATO

Paul Cornish

Contents

The first half of 1997 was a lively time for NATO. Its diplomatic outreach led to the signature of the NATO–Russia Founding Act, the creation of the Permanent Joint Council and the Euro-Atlantic Partnership Council, and the development of its existing Partnership for Peace programme. The Czech Republic, Hungary and Poland were invited to begin accession negotiations.

NATO also continued its programme of internal adaptation – a complex scheme to reconfigure its command and control structure and its force posture. This lucid study focuses upon these inner workings of the Alliance. The author describes four 'paths to compromise' (US, British, French and German), without which the complex formulae devised in 1996 and 1997 could not have been agreed. The study concludes that NATO, as an 'alliance of choice', has finally established its ground in the new European security order.

Dr Paul Cornish is a lecturer in Defence Studies at King's College London, and is a member of the Defence Studies Department, Joint Services Command and Staff College, Bracknell.

144pp
ISBN 1 85567 466 1
(hbk)
ISBN 1 85567 467 X
(pbk)

December 1997   RIIA/Pinter   £27.50/£11.99

Chatham House Papers — THE ROYAL INSTITUTE OF INTERNATIONAL AFFAIRS

The World Trade Organization
Constitution and Jurisprudence

John H. Jackson

Professor Jackson's *Restructuring the GATT System* (Chatham House Papers, 1990) played an influential role in stimulating debate on the overhaul of the constitution and institutional structures of the GATT. That debate gave rise to the World Trade Organization, which is now faced with a raft of new policy challenges. In this new study, Professor Jackson discusses the strengths and limitations of the WTO and how it will need to adapt to meet new demands, focusing on the constitutional structure and the dispute settlement procedures. The text is supplemented by a number of useful appendices.

'No one has a better understanding of the evolution of world trade law and the WTO as an organization than does John Jackson.' – *Warren Lavorel, Deputy Director General of WTO*

'This is, in my opinion, the most authoritative comment published until now on the institutional results of the Uruguay Round negotiations and the one which trade negotiators and practitioners have been looking for.' – *Hugo Paemen, Ambassador for the European Union to the United States, and Negotiator for the European Community in the Uruguay Round.*

John H. Jackson joined the Faculty of Law at Georgetown University, Washington DC, in January 1998, and is an emeritus professor of law at the University of Michigan. He has a worldwide reputation as a leading authority on international trade law.

128pp ISBN 1 85567 352 5 (hbk), 1 85567 353 3 (pbk)

April 1998   RIIA/Pinter   £27.50/£11.99